As you step forward into the next chapter of your life, carry this truth with you. You are the author of your story and have the power to decide what comes next, with the strength to rewrite the parts that no longer serve you and create an exciting future. Moreover, you have the courage to take the first step, however small, toward building the life you truly want.

No more waiting. No more shrinking yourself to fit into spaces not built for you. It's time to dream bigger, step into your power, and create your own table reflecting your worth, your vision, and your limitless potential.

Heather Dolland Tamam

CREATE YOUR OWN TABLE

A GUIDE TO DISCOVERING YOUR PURPOSE

HEATHER DOLLAND TAMAM

Published By

DOLTAM CREATIVE SOLUTIONS

www.doltam.com

CREATE YOUR OWN TABLE
A GUIDE TO DISCOVERING YOUR PURPOSE

Doltam Creative Solutions
www.doltam.com

Book Cover Photo by Sharon Daniels Studio

Library of Congress Control Number: 2025909383

ISBN PAPERBACK: 979-8-9987323-1-7

ISBN HARDCOVER: 979-8-9987323-0-0

ALSO, BY
HEATHER DOLLAND TAMAM

Discovering The New York Craft Spirits
Boom

Before The Glass

Things To Consider When Entering The
Booze Business

Pivot

Because Life Doesn't Always Go As Planned

DEDICATON

To Amos. Thank you for holding space to allow me to grow and discover all of who I am. Your steady support allows me to show up fully and become the best version of myself.

TABLE OF CONTENTS

INTRODUCTION

WHY THIS? WHY NOW?

I began writing this book two months after I shot the cover. What can I say? It's just part of my creative process. I discovered some time ago that inspiration often comes from unexpected places. The cover, in its conception, wasn't just an image; it was a silent conversation between my inner self and the creative spirit I carried within me. I looked at it and let it "speak" to me, asking myself: *What would I expect to read if I picked up a book that looked like this?* A simple image of me, in black and white, inviting you as the reader to add any nuances from your own mind's eye. It's in this way that our stories can intermingle from the start.

There's something profoundly compelling about how a visual has the power to ignite a creative fire. When I captured the image for the cover, I wasn't simply taking a photograph; I was capturing a moment in time, a fragment of emotion, a thought that would later define the very essence of this book. At every stage in life, the

1

true value of the moment we're in is only truly appreciated later on; knowing this, I remain mindful of the people around me and trust the person who captured the image immensely. Sharon took my very first author's picture 10 years ago, and I've trusted her to capture the true essence of who I am—at every stage—ever since.

I've also come to appreciate that a book is more than words on paper as a multi-sensory experience: a merging of thoughts, emotions, and ideas inviting the reader to step into another world. When I finally sat down to write on February 4, 2025—a day that felt both ordinary and extraordinary—the wider world was in a state of flux, significant shifts occurring both in the United States and abroad.

An undercurrent of uncertainty, of change, rippled through communities and industries alike as massive layoffs in both the private and public sectors made headlines—affecting hundreds of thousands of lives. People were feeling the weight of economic and social transitions, and the pain was palpable. Yet amid this turbulence, something unexpected happened in my own little corner of the creative world. Two of my YouTube posts—most notably *How to Build Credibility Without Credentials*—began to gain traction, one post after another resonating with an audience hungry for guidance and authenticity. As views soared and comments poured in, I realized my message had touched a nerve as a reminder that credibility isn't just about formal qualifications but about the genuine value we bring to our work. The viral nature of that particular post was both humbling and enlightening. In the digital age where content is king, *context* is queen. YouTube's algorithm, designed to curate content based on individual interests, had aligned my message with the needs of those seeking practical wisdom in uncertain times. The idea that "your job is not your identity" struck a chord with many, prompting an outpouring of support, questions, and personal stories from viewers.

I began to see how an amalgamation of timing, technology, and authentic experience was creating a perfect storm, with messages not only heard but truly *understood*. It was then that I recognized the importance of sharing my purpose in these same moments as a source of good and a guiding light for those searching for clarity and direction: the entire premise my company Doltam Creative Solutions is built upon.

One pivotal decision I made early on in my journey to complete this book was to leverage technology in a way that honored my natural rhythm. Never really a fan of typing, I knew my thoughts would flow more freely when I spoke them aloud and thus turned to speech-to-text software to capture my ideas: a decision born out of practicality and the ability to articulate my ideas faster than I could via writing.

WHY THIS? WHY NOW?

At the core of this book lies a simple yet powerful message: create meaningful content. It may sound straightforward but isn't always in a world inundated with noise and the superficial, and I very much wanted to create something primed to resonate on a deeper level and stand the test of time. Creating meaningful content isn't a one-off task; it's a continuous process involving reflection, adaptation, and growth. It means looking inward to discover your unique perspective and then sharing the same with the world in a way that inspires others to as well. It's about understanding that every story, every insight, and every lesson learned is a thread in the rich tapestry of human experience; threads woven together with intention and care form a narrative that's both transformative and timeless.

One day while recording, I was struck by a realization: I was repeating things I'd said numerous times before, something unavoidable when you're sharing lived experience. This book is, after all, primarily the story of my life. I also had the realization that quality content can be "repackaged" and adapted for multiple purposes. While it may seem obvious to others, I was simply not familiar with the fact that authors adapt knowledge in this way to rapidly bring a book to market. I'm sharing this as your very first tip (prior to Chapter 1, in fact!) as I don't believe in sitting on valuable information and it's something that absolutely works.

Meaningful content, in its truest form, is an investment in oneself and one's community. It's about taking the time to explore ideas, dig beneath the surface, and present insights that are both authentic and actionable. Creating content rich in purpose builds a bridge of trust with your audience, who in turn begin to view you as not just a creator but a guide—someone who's navigated the complexities of life and emerged with wisdom worth sharing on the other side. Never has this been truer than in our rapidly changing world where the shelf life of information continues to shrink by the day. What was relevant yesterday is often obsolete tomorrow, and the pace of innovation shows no signs of slowing down. Social media, instant communication, and artificial intelligence have accelerated this timeline, making us feel as if we're falling behind before we even start. But I digress...

With the experience of writing a trio of books already under my belt, I put my head down and focused on writing what I'd already deemed my most important book to date—feeling a particular sense of urgency to get this done immediately. Failing to plant the seed now would leave nothing to harvest. Period. For whatever reason, farming and taking the right action in the right season came to mind. Our creative pursuits, likewise, require careful timing, deliberate action, and a willingness to persevere through both fertile seasons and barren ones: a metaphor that extends beyond the realm of creativity into every aspect of life including our careers, relationships, and personal growth.

Many people lament not having the time to [insert excuse here], but do those individuals ever sit down and calculate the cost of lost opportunities? What has *not* taking action cost you? Some of us live in extended wintertime hibernation simply because we never take the time to consider seasons exist in life as well as nature. The fact that you picked up this book means there's a good chance you're feeling as if you've been living on unyielding barren land and are ready for change—but don't know where to start. As in nature, you must perform the right action(s) in the right season(s) to reap the fruit of your labor; I hope this book provides you with the clarity necessary to do so in alignment with the vision you have for your life.

As I mentioned before, everything I share is my own lived experience. As an avid reader and constant pursuer of knowledge, I set aside just as much time to learn (with the help of courses and coaches) as I do to mentor and teach. My life—a series of constant evolutions teaching many valuable lessons—has seen me pursue careers in different industries and make decisions others find unfathomable. Primarily driving me? The pursuit of happiness. Evolving into my current space, I began to recognize the value of my knowledge and how (when combined with my desire to serve and live a purpose-driven life) I can meaningfully contribute to the lives of those around me.

In the chapters that follow, I'll provide you with the tools and strategies I've personally leaned on to create my own table. Allow me explain this metaphor...

For years, I lived professionally frustrated: an emotion I made peace with and accepted until I realized I was making a *choice* rather than a *decision*. Have you ever had a vison those around you don't understand nor support? The constant feeling that your purpose is being questioned? It took some time, but I eventually realized people sometimes simply won't see nor understand your vision not because it's wrong but because it's ahead of its time; sometimes, rejection is redirection. These visions are placed in you, not others. Why become frustrated while waiting for them to align themselves with what you're doing? Rather than waiting for them to offer you a seat at their table, whatever that looks like, why not simply create your *own*?

In hindsight, I realized the prior sequence of events significantly impacted my results, taking us back to the question of seasons and taking the right action at the right time. Everything you need is already within, waiting to emerge when given the opportunity; *you* are the source.

Before we begin, please remember this is my own story and evolution into the world of entrepreneurship. I'm by no means a business expert, nor do I hold an MBA. Everything I share I've *lived*, experience teaching me that if you want to know the path ahead ask someone who's coming back. Gone are the days of seeking advice from people who haven't, been where I'm desirous of going. This is precisely why I'm sharing my very own journey as a source of clarity and direction. Though I don't know you, I have a sneaking suspicion something is stirring within to make you believe your journey is imminent; you wouldn't have picked up this book otherwise.

I have no idea what you're seeking but do know every journey begins with a first step. Thank you for allowing me to be part of yours. Thank you for trusting that what I share is a message you want to receive as the difference you need to push forward. Believe in yourself, knowing it's so easy to simply *not* take action. We give ourselves more than enough reasons to not do something and stay comfortable—ignoring the reasons we should—so let's go ahead and acknowledge (and celebrate!) that you've taken the first step. After all, actions celebrated are actions repeated!

CHAPTER 1

LOOKING BACK TO MOVE FORWARD

I was in the middle of a Zoom meeting, enjoying a beautiful summer afternoon in East Hampton, NY, when it hit me: I was going to write a new book.

The day stands out in my memory because the meeting was part of a course I was taking to improve my communication. Part of the exercise on that particular day was to share something we genuinely did not want to do but likewise recognized as important for our growth. The thought process behind the activity? The thing you want to avoid is likely the very thing you must do to stretch yourself and facilitate your transformation.

In that moment, I (begrudgingly) mentioned writing a new book in response to the question at hand and distinctly remember feeling my stomach quite literally turn. It'd only been a year since I published *Pivot: Because Life Doesn't Always Go As Planned*, and I really wasn't in the mood to embark on a second book-writing journey quite so soon; but as my coach so eloquently said, "Irritation is the first step toward transformation." I knew writing this book would likewise play out as a critical part of my journey.

The irony of me writing and publishing *Pivot*, meanwhile, is that my life did in fact pivot as a result. For those of you unfamiliar with my story, my last book was a means to share struggles I've overcome both professionally and personally throughout my life—an attempt to give readers glimpses into my own personal narrative that I hadn't shared in previous books.

An environmental consultant of 15 years back then, I had a parallel career as a brand ambassador in the alcohol industry: a side hustle that opened the door to launching my business supporting craft distillers. Along came COVID, though, and its corresponding impacts; after my clients lost half of their accounts seemingly overnight, I eventually made the decision to apply my extensive knowledge to content creation.

Most of the content I initially created focused on making cocktail recipes for different occasions, which was easy enough since I had what felt like an endless supply of products on hand from all the brands I'd worked with. Since all of our lives had shifted online, moreover, it made sense to engage in an aspect of marketing I hadn't previously had time to focus on. As my content began to gain traction, I realized I could engage with a *multitude* of brands—not only those in the alcohol space.

One of the aspects I loved most about content creation was the freedom it gave me to engage with a wide range of industries and brands. I was no longer brand or industry agnostic—my work spanned everything from wellness to beauty, food, travel, and what we typically refer to as "lifestyle" content. It was dynamic, creative, and exciting. But over time, despite the enjoyment and flexibility it offered, I began to feel an unexpected void. Life was objectively good—I was home most of the day, filming and editing content for brands I genuinely admired. But something deeper was missing.

The truth is, the work wasn't feeding my soul.

It felt increasingly clear that I had far too much knowledge, experience, and insight stored in my mind to confine my days to curating polished photos and videos. Don't get me wrong—being an artist is an incredible gift. But I've never considered myself one. The natural eye and instinct that many photographers and visual creators possess is not something I inherently have. Every tool in my creative toolkit is a learned skill—acquired through years of trial, error, and a steady education from what I call "YouTube University."

In fact, I fell into content creation entirely by accident. A brand I genuinely used and loved saw a TikTok I had

11

casually made featuring their product and reached out. That unexpected moment opened a new door, and before I knew it, I was creating content professionally. But in the spirit of transparency, let me be clear: I don't consider myself a traditional photographer or videographer. My creations are built on passion, practicality, and purpose—not perfection.

And that's where the shift began. I realized I wanted more than to *create content*—I wanted to *create change*.

After spending a couple of years as a content creator and lifestyle model, I felt the need to reconnect with a deeper part of myself—one that wasn't curated for brand campaigns or camera angles. That desire led me to write my third book, *Pivot: Because Life Doesn't Always Go As Planned*. By that time, I had fully stepped away from both the alcohol and environmental industries, two chapters of my professional life that had shaped me significantly but no longer aligned with the direction I felt called to explore.

I had come to realize that I wanted to share more of *me*—not just the polished, publicly visible version, but the full, well-rounded person behind the lens. The one who had weathered unexpected detours, professional reinventions, and personal growth. I knew I had a calling stirring inside me, though I couldn't yet articulate what it was. I only knew it involved making meaning out of everything I had lived through.

At the time, *Pivot* existed only as a series of disconnected Word documents on my laptop—chapters I'd written over time but couldn't figure out how to weave into a cohesive story. The narrative felt fragmented, and I wasn't sure how to pull it all together. That clarity came unexpectedly, during lunch with a college friend I hadn't seen in years.

As we caught up over Greek salads and glasses of sauvignon blanc, he told me something that stopped me in my tracks: advice I had casually given him two decades earlier—something I barely remembered—had completely shifted the course of his professional life. Hearing that gave me goosebumps. And as I explained that I felt I was finally moving in the right direction, even if I still didn't know exactly where I was headed, a light bulb went off.

In that moment, I saw the thread running through every one of my seemingly disjointed chapters: the quiet, persistent power of taking small, consistent action, even when the outcome is uncertain. That became the heartbeat of *Pivot*, and the message I knew I was meant to share.

Many people miss the significance of this statement, assuming that achieving anything of significance requires taking gargantuan swings. *Direction*, however, is more important than *speed*, so small, consistent steps in the right direction will ultimately get you to your desired destination.

A few months after *Pivot* was released, I began taking a closer look at the feedback I was receiving from readers. I wasn't just reading their comments—I was listening for the deeper messages embedded within their words. And slowly, a pattern began to emerge, one that echoed a familiar theme I had encountered across all of my business ventures: the idea of a "gap." It became clear that the common thread in my entrepreneurial journey was my ability to identify a missing piece—whether in an industry, a system, or a mindset—and then set out to fill it. That, it turned out, was my zone of genius.

The more I listened, the more I noticed that the majority of responses I was getting were from women aged 40 and up, most of them in their 50s. They came from different backgrounds, yet shared three powerful commonalities that deeply resonated with me. First, they expressed a sense of frustration—having spent decades supporting the dreams of others while putting their own aspirations on hold. Second, they failed to see the value in their past experiences, overlooking how their knowledge, skills, and stories were not only valid but transferable to new paths. And third, many had no experience with online platforms or content creation, which made them feel like it was simply too late to try something new. That belief—that their time had passed—was the most heartbreaking of all.

These revelations didn't just tug at my heart; they activated something in me. I realized I was being presented with an opportunity to fill yet another gap—not one rooted in branding or digital content, but one centered on purpose, possibility, and reinvention. That was the moment the mission of Doltam Creative Solutions began to shift. What had started as a platform to showcase my content creation services evolved into a purpose-driven space dedicated to helping individuals—particularly women in midlife—who were ready for change but didn't know how or where to begin.

From that insight, a new direction—and a new company mantra—was born: *"You don't need a business plan. You need a starting point."* Because what most people are really looking for isn't permission or perfection—they just need a path. And I knew I could help them find it.

Absolutely all of my experiences came together here—arming me with the tools necessary to serve the sector I knew intimately. I recognized myself in so many reader comments, realizing they were all at different stages within the same journey.

It was then that I recalled these words: "Your purpose unfolds when you take the first step in the direction of your purpose. Don't be worried about perfect alignment, take steps in the right direction."

With this in mind, I began pondering challenges I'd experienced and how I overcame them and knew I could create elegant solutions to show others how to do the same. In immediately deciding to create programs to do just that, I considered emotions I'd worked past and focused on the most important components of meaningful change.

Much of what holds us back has less to do with the knowledge we possess and more to do with the fear of not being *enough* nor qualified. Often accompanying this is a sense of embarrassment that we aren't on a level playing field with others and the belief that we're simply not smart enough, so easy to fall victim to the thief of comparison and perceptions that we can't add value. Nothing could be further from the truth! The challenge, likewise, is that very few people realize the uniqueness of their voice and that when people forge connections with others, they're connecting with the person more so than the message.

I remember joining a networking group years ago, young and new to the concept. I was an environmental consultant at the time, shifting from my role as a scientist to business development, and needed to hone my networking skills. The head of the group told me something I'll never forget: "Heather, there's really not much difference between the company you work for and other companies that offer the same service. What's different is *you*. People want to work with people they like. They want to work with people they trust. More importantly, though, they want to work with people they believe will work with their best interest in mind."

The reason I'm sharing this with you is because I need you to remember—*really* remember—that everything you need is already within you. That may sound cliché, but it's the absolute truth. You weren't meant to chase someone else's blueprint. You were designed with a unique combination of lived experiences, insights, instincts, and talents that no one else on this planet possesses. You might be surprised how often we forget that. How often we discredit our own voice simply because it's familiar to us.

Yes, there may be quite literally a million people out there doing what you *think* you want to do—writing books, launching courses, building businesses, coaching others, leading workshops, designing products, whatever your "it" may be. But here's the truth: *not a single one of them can do it the way you can*. They don't have your story. They haven't walked your path. They can't see through your lens or feel through your heart. They cannot connect with others in the same way you can because, quite simply, *they're not you*.

So don't fall for the lie that "anyone can do it." That idea—that you're just another face in the crowd—isn't just wrong, it's dangerous. It's the kind of thinking that keeps gifted people playing small. And something tells me that if you're reading this, you've already played that role long enough. You've probably been the one who steps in after someone else dropped the ball—cleaning up the mess, fixing what was broken, delivering excellence behind the scenes without ever demanding recognition. You've been the one others depend on to make things right. So no, not everyone *can* do what you do—not with your standards, your touch, your insight, or your intention.

The problem is, we often underestimate the value of our own circle of influence. We convince ourselves that we're not ready because we don't have 10,000 followers or a giant email list. But the truth is, you don't need to go viral or be seen by the masses to begin. You don't need to wait for "permission" or visibility or perfect conditions. You just need to start—*right where you are*, with *who* you are, and with *what* you know.

Start with one person. One meaningful interaction. One piece of content. One message. One offering. One connection.

The key word here is *meaningful*. Impact is not measured by quantity—it's measured by depth. If you truly want to create your own table and forge your own

18

path, it's likely because you know, deep down, that what you've learned along your journey has value. And while the people around you might not always see it—might not always affirm it or understand it—you do. You know. That alone is enough reason to begin.

Creating your own table isn't about building something grand for the world to admire. It's about building something real—something honest, something that reflects your truth and holds space for others who need what only you can offer. It's about choosing not to shrink just because the people in your current environment can't fully grasp your greatness.

So don't wait for external validation. Don't wait for a crowd to cheer you on. The very act of taking that first step—no matter how small—is a declaration that your voice matters. That your experience matters. That *you* matter.

Because you do.

And the moment you choose to believe that? That's the moment your table begins to take shape.

CHAPTER 2

DO YOU BELIEVE IT BECAUSE IT'S THE TRUTH, OR IS IT THE TRUTH BECAUSE YOU BELIEVE IT?

So many of us never question our beliefs as they're simply ingrained in us. Most people, after all, don't stop and think to themselves: *Why do I believe this? Why do I think this way?* So often when we begin to question our beliefs, it's because we realize if we want to go where we've never been, we must do things we've never done. When that time arrives, conflict and friction can run rampant as the people around us may not understand our desire for change: not grasping our need for something new and/or perhaps taking it personally, seeing our desire for change or improvement as a personal rejection or insult.

Each of us carries an internal blueprint—a deeply rooted map of how we see ourselves and what we believe is possible for our lives. That blueprint is shaped by our belief system, which has been forming since childhood through experiences, relationships, culture, religion, education, and repeated narratives. And while we all have the capacity to grow and revise our internal wiring, the hard truth is this: much of the advice we receive from those closest to us is not based on what's best *for us*, but rather what feels safest *for them*.

I know that sounds a bit harsh, but stay with me.

When people who love us offer guidance, it often comes from a well-meaning place. They want to protect us from disappointment, heartache, failure, or financial instability. They care deeply—but their perspective is filtered through their own fears, limitations, and life experiences. So, when they suggest a path for us, it's often one that keeps us neatly tucked inside a comfort zone they're familiar with—a box they've either lived in themselves or one they believe is "reasonable" or "secure."

But here's the thing: if you're trying to shift your life in a meaningful way—if you're trying to break generational patterns, shatter financial ceilings, start something entirely new, or step into your purpose—*tiny moves inside tiny boxes simply won't cut it*. Playing small will not get you to big results.

DO YOU BELIEVE IT BECAUSE IT'S THE TRUTH, OR IS IT THE TRUTH BECAUSE YOU BELIEVE IT?

This is something I see often with clients. They come to me feeling stuck, frustrated, and confused because they've been seeking advice from people who love them—but who don't *see* the vision that's been planted in their hearts. And I always remind them: *your vision is yours*. It wasn't gifted to your spouse, your parents, your siblings, your best friend, or your coworkers. It was placed within *you*—and that alone makes it sacred and valid.

Now, I want to be clear—I'm not suggesting you lie to your loved ones or isolate yourself. But I *am* suggesting you use discernment when choosing who gets a front-row seat to your evolution. When you're in the vulnerable, uncertain stage of growing into your next chapter, it's easy to doubt yourself. And when someone you love or admire echoes that doubt, it can hit harder than you expected. Their words can reinforce the very fears you're trying to unlearn. The inner critic already lives rent-free in your mind—you don't need external voices turning up its volume.

That's why I recommend protecting your vision in the early stages. Guard it the way you would a delicate seed you just planted. Water it quietly. Nurture it intentionally. Let it take root before you invite too many opinions in. There will be a time for sharing—when you're more grounded and your confidence has had time to solidify. But in the meantime, focus on building trust with yourself.

Because as you grow, not everyone will understand your choices. Not everyone will cheer. And that's okay. You're not building a life based on their fears—you're building one based on your potential.

So honor your blueprint. Challenge what no longer serves you. Make bold moves outside the box, and give yourself permission to evolve, even when it's uncomfortable.

Because the life you're trying to create? It's not meant to be small. And neither are you.

From a professional standpoint, have you reached a point in your career where it feels like you've checked every box? You've taken advantage of the opportunities presented to you, climbed the corporate ladder, earned the promotions, collected the accolades—and yet, somehow, you still feel stuck. You've done everything "right," followed the expected path, and made the most of what was available. And yet, you're bumping up against a ceiling that just won't give—no matter how hard you push.

If this resonates, know this: *you are not alone.* I've been there—more than once, in fact. I know what it feels like to be seen as successful on paper but still feel like you're missing something vital. That invisible weight, that lingering question: *Is this really it?*

In many cases, what you're feeling is more than burnout or boredom. It may be something deeper—a block. You may have heard this term before in conversations about energy, emotions, or finances. A block is essentially an internal obstruction that limits your ability to move forward, thrive, or expand—no matter how much effort you're putting in.

Let's break it down.

An **energy block** refers to a disruption in the natural flow of your personal energy. You may find yourself feeling emotionally drained, unmotivated, overwhelmed, or even physically unwell—yet unable to pinpoint why. It's often rooted in unprocessed experiences, unresolved trauma, or environments that no longer align with who you're becoming.

A **financial block**, on the other hand, typically stems from deeply ingrained beliefs about money—many of which you may not even be aware of. These can include subconscious narratives like "I'm not good with money," "I'll never make more than I need," or "People like me don't get rich." These beliefs often originate in childhood, past experiences, or cultural conditioning and create invisible barriers to receiving, managing, or growing your financial resources.

24

DO YOU BELIEVE IT BECAUSE IT'S THE TRUTH, OR IS IT THE TRUTH BECAUSE YOU BELIEVE IT?

What's most frustrating is that these blocks can persist even when you're doing all the "right" things. You've taken courses, read the books, made the connections—but the results don't match the effort. That's because these blocks don't respond to logic. They're embedded in your internal programming, and unless they're acknowledged and reworked, they'll continue to sabotage your progress.

For years, I understood this intellectually—especially when it came to finances. I'd read about money mindsets, limiting beliefs, and abundance theory. But recently, I uncovered something that shifted everything for me. It wasn't just a new strategy or another mindset tip—it was a deeper revelation that helped me see where I'd unknowingly been standing in my own way. It changed how I show up in my work, how I relate to money, and how I guide others through the process of breaking free.

Please allow me to share it with you...

I was at a public-speaking coaching conference, attending a learning session focused on different speaking techniques, when I was about to tell a story I'd repeated often and was honestly quite sick of. Just as I was about to present, I changed my mind at the 99th hour and decided to go with a different story I believed was more interesting—one describing a low point in my life. If you read my book *Pivot: Because Life Doesn't*

DO YOU BELIEVE IT BECAUSE IT'S THE TRUTH, OR IS IT
THE TRUTH BECAUSE YOU BELIEVE IT?

Always Go As Planned, you may recall how I'd made a
super quick decision to buy a home: getting the idea in
April 2003 and receiving the keys that September. That
was the fun part. Then my ceiling collapsed... twice. It
was part of the story I'd share that day.

*"I remember walking through the door and smelling the
distinct odor of mold, something that jumps out at you
when you have sheetrock saturated with water. I ran
upstairs, and sure enough, the ceiling had collapsed
onto my bed—for the second time! As if that wasn't
enough, the water had run down the side of the house
and impacted the ceiling on the first floor as well. I was
probably about 31 years old at the time and had no idea
that insurance isn't fond of you actually calling them
with a claim, apparently. It would be my second claim in
two years, but I had no choice as I didn't have the
money to fix my roof again. Two months after that
debacle, I went downstairs and discovered the boiler
had broken—pumping 25 gallons of water into my
basement for three straight days until I was able to get it
fixed. I'd had enough. It was time to sell.*

*I already knew I wanted to live in New York City, so why
prolong the torment? When I visited the offices in my
town to get the necessary documents to put my home
on the market, however, guess what I discovered? My
house, even though I was the third owner, did not have a
certificate of occupancy. Go figure! My house had been*

built in 1954, and all of this was happening in 2009—55 years later! Turns out, the structure had been physically moved from one part of the property to the other. I'm guessing because this is such a rare and unusual occurrence, what was on file (and apparently misinterpreted) was the certificate of said move not the certificate of occupancy—the most basic requirement of any residence.

This headache meant I needed a survey of the entire property, which was precisely when I discovered my fence wasn't in the right place and had to be moved. THEN I got a call from the insurance company and learned an inspector had been by and determined my siding wasn't in good shape, putting my insurance coverage at risk; they'd either triple my premium or drop me completely if I didn't replace the siding covering my entire house, which would cost in the neighborhood of twenty thousand dollars if I'm remembering correctly. Talk about feeling overwhelmed! The American Dream? I think not. It felt like everything and everyone had turned against me, and I was living in a financial nightmare."

It was the first time I'd shared that particular story, and it involved practicing what's referred to as a "sentence stem" used to transition from one part of a story to another within a speech. My stem was said as follows: *"And then I believed that by playing big, I'd incur big financial responsibilities; so I decided to play small instead."* I spoke these words with as much casual ease as you likely just did while reading them before going on to say, *"This is precisely the reason why I created my business: to support individuals who face their own difficulties amidst challenging transitions."*

Two days later, I was in the middle of a Zoom meeting—sharing the art of telling a story that connects as I retold the story—when I felt the earth move beneath me, realizing that the previously mentioned incidents in fact validated the belief I'd shared in my sentence stem. I couldn't believe it. Not a general statement, it was one backed by the emotion associated with each of those experiences. The looming financial mental block I was facing at the time was one of my own making; I'd created my own belief.

When I eventually moved to New York City, I remember feeling a sense of immense relief—as though I were leaving behind a chapter of my life that had grown far too heavy to carry. I wasn't just moving to a new city; I was purging the weight of homeownership, the bills, the constant upkeep, the stress, and all the responsibilities that came with it. I was done with it. I told myself I never wanted to be burdened with those things again. And I meant it.

At the time, it felt like liberation. But in that exalted moment of release—driven by emotion, frustration, and exhaustion—I didn't recognize the power behind my words. Nor did I realize the energetic weight they carried. What I had declared so firmly, what I had spoken with such conviction, wasn't just a decision. It was a vow—one that was saturated in negative emotion and, unknowingly, charged with energetic consequence.

I'm sharing this not just to tell you my "house" story, but to illustrate something bigger. We all have our own version of this—a moment in time that, on the surface, may seem insignificant or even justified, but that quietly took root in our belief system. It might be tied to a job, a relationship, a city, a financial situation, or even something someone said to you in passing. These moments become turning points, shaping our perception of what's possible and quietly guiding our future decisions, often without our awareness.

The truth is, when experiences are charged with emotion, especially negative ones, they leave a much deeper imprint. And it wasn't until much later that I realized just how deeply I had absorbed those chaotic household experiences—how they'd become woven into the fabric of my subconscious. I had created an emotional association between homeownership and struggle. Between stability and stress. And every time the idea of buying property came up again, my body would tighten, my spirit would resist, and I couldn't

quite understand why—until I traced it back to the vows
I'd unknowingly made.

The irony is, I was hyper-aware of many of the more
obvious financial blocks: things like "making money is
hard," "rich people are selfish," or "money is the root of
all evil." We've all heard these before. I'd done the work
to reject them and stay vigilant when they crept in. But
this was different. This wasn't someone else's belief.
This was mine—one I had created in a moment of
survival, without realizing its long-term effects.

And that's the tricky part. We often talk about guarding
our minds against limiting beliefs from the outside
world—society, family, media, culture. But what
happens when the most powerful limitations come
from within? When they're born of our own lived
experiences, wrapped in emotional pain and disguised
as common sense or self-protection?

That's when healing and unlearning become even more
critical. Because it's one thing to spot a harmful belief
when it doesn't belong to you. It's another to recognize
and dismantle one that you *built*—one that has become
part of your identity. But here's the good news: once you
become aware of it, you gain the power to release it. To
rewrite it. To consciously create a new story—one that
supports the life you truly want.

DO YOU BELIEVE IT BECAUSE IT'S THE TRUTH, OR IS IT THE TRUTH BECAUSE YOU BELIEVE IT?

Once I realized just how much of a chokehold my mental block had on my progress—financially, professionally, and emotionally—I knew I had to address it *immediately*. This wasn't a "maybe later" situation. It was a *stat* moment. So I turned to something that had always intrigued me but that I hadn't fully committed to: meditation.

As I began exploring different approaches to quiet my mind and reconnect with myself, I stumbled upon something that would radically shift my understanding of personal transformation. It happened unexpectedly—while listening to an episode of the *Know Thyself* podcast, hosted by Andre Duqum. The episode was titled **"Reprogram Your Limiting Beliefs While You Sleep & Design Your Destiny"**, and it featured none other than Dr. Bruce Lipton, a renowned cellular biologist whose work bridges science and spirituality in a way that is both grounded and deeply inspiring.

Talk about divine timing.

The episode lasted 2 hours and 20 minutes, and after the first listen, I was so moved, I played it again immediately. I sat with it, journaled, let it sink in. Those 4 hours and 40 minutes were—without exaggeration—some of the most transformative of my life.

DO YOU BELIEVE IT BECAUSE IT'S THE TRUTH, OR IS IT THE TRUTH BECAUSE YOU BELIEVE IT?

Dr. Lipton explained how our belief systems are formed during the earliest years of our development. Between birth and age seven, our brains exist primarily in a **Theta state**, a brainwave frequency that functions much like hypnosis. In this state, children aren't reasoning or questioning what they hear—they're *absorbing*. Downloading every message, every behavior, every tone, every emotional nuance from parents, caregivers, teachers, and the world around them. They take everything in, unfiltered, because they haven't yet developed the mental tools to distinguish truth from bias, fear from fact, love from control.

Dr. Lipton emphasized an ancient truth, echoing the wisdom of Aristotle: *"Give me a child until he is seven, and I will show you the man."* That statement hit me like a thunderbolt. It suddenly made sense why so many of us unknowingly repeat the same emotional patterns, money habits, or relationship dynamics we witnessed as children. We grow up, but those early scripts remain—replaying in the background, influencing our decisions without us even realizing it.

It's the reason we hear echoes of our parents in our own voices. The reason we sometimes sabotage progress just as success is within reach. The reason we unconsciously gravitate toward familiar patterns, even if they no longer serve us.

But here's the part that changed everything for me: just because these beliefs were programmed into us, doesn't mean they can't be reprogrammed.

This is where hope, empowerment, and real possibility come in.

Dr. Lipton shared that the subconscious mind is incredibly receptive to new messages during specific windows—especially during the Theta state, which also occurs naturally when we are drifting off to sleep and during the early moments of waking. That means we can *literally* rewrite our internal programming by consistently exposing ourselves to new, empowering beliefs—particularly through audio recordings designed to target the subconscious. Listening to these recordings while sleeping allows the messages to bypass conscious resistance and settle into the subconscious mind, replacing outdated stories with new truths.

I know, it sounds a little out there. I had the same reaction at first. But the science behind it is sound, and more importantly, I've experienced the results for myself. If you're still with me, I want you to hear this clearly: this works. But only if you're open to it.

This is the kind of tool that can change the trajectory of your life—not because it's flashy or trendy, but because it meets you where transformation begins: *at the root*. If you take nothing else from this book, take this. Your life is not fixed. Your blocks are not permanent. You have the ability to rewire your mind, rewrite your story, and reimagine what's possible.

All it takes is the willingness to believe that change is possible—and the commitment to start, one night at a time.

So now I was off to the races—fired up and determined to figure out how to actually *execute* this newfound mission of rewiring my subconscious mind. I'd had my breakthrough moment. Now came the work of integrating it into my life.

Have you ever noticed how, after buying a new car, you suddenly see that same exact Toyota or Audi model everywhere? It's not that those cars just appeared overnight—it's that your awareness shifted. Your mind became attuned to what was always there. That's exactly what started happening to me. Once I downloaded a meditation app and began diving into the world of self-development, it felt like I had unlocked a whole universe of information that had been hiding in plain sight. It wasn't necessarily *new* information—it was just new *to me*.

As I began exploring more deeply, I discovered something that immediately caught my attention: long-form affirmation audio files, often 8 to 11 hours in length, specifically designed to be listened to *while you sleep*. That part—the overnight listening—was key. Here's why.

As adults, we naturally cycle in and out of various brainwave states throughout the day and night. Right before falling asleep and again in the early morning hours, our brains enter what's called the Theta state—a brainwave frequency associated with deep relaxation, heightened suggestibility, creativity, intuition, and memory integration. It's the same state children are predominantly in for the first seven years of life—when beliefs, behaviors, and worldviews are most easily formed and absorbed.

This is why Theta is the sweet spot for subconscious reprogramming.

Listening to affirmations or guided messages while you sleep isn't just a feel-good habit—it's a *scientifically supported strategy* that leverages your natural brain rhythms to overwrite limiting beliefs and reinforce new, empowering ones. But here's something important I want to stress, especially if this idea feels a little out of your comfort zone:

You are always in control.

I once had a conversation with someone who was deeply resistant to the idea of sleep programming. They were concerned that listening to something while unconscious would make them vulnerable, as if they were handing their mind over to an outside force. But here's the truth: you have the power to choose *what* you listen to. You're not surrendering your autonomy— you're using it in a powerful, intentional way.

In fact, if you want to take full control of the process, you can record your own affirmations. You don't need fancy equipment or a studio setup. You have everything you need in the palm of your hand—your phone.

Here's what I suggest if you're curious about trying this for yourself:

- Decide what you want to reinforce. Is it self-worth? Financial abundance? Confidence? Clarity? Peace?

- Write a script or collect affirmations that reflect the beliefs you want to internalize. You can use powerful paragraphs from books you love, or simply compile a list of affirmations that speak directly to your goals.

- Record yourself reading them aloud. Don't worry about sounding perfect—this is for your ears only. Speak with intention and emotion.

- Make the recording at least 30 minutes long, or up to an hour if you'd like. Then set it to loop or repeat throughout the night.

- Play it every night—preferably with a headset or a speaker by your bedside. Personally, I use a wired headset—though it's not the best option if you tend to move around in your sleep—as a way to avoid disturbing anyone else nearby. Even at a low volume, the affirmations are still incredibly effective.

As with any practice, consistency is key. Give yourself a minimum of 21 days—the widely accepted timeframe for forming a new habit or internalizing a belief. Some shifts may happen quickly. Others will unfold over time. But with each night, your mind will begin to receive a different message—one that supports, empowers, and elevates you.

This isn't magic. It's intention paired with neuroscience. And it's a tool that can truly transform your inner landscape—if you're open enough to try it.

This exercise truly worked wonders for me. To my surprise, within just *three days* of starting it, I uncovered and removed a completely different block—one I hadn't even been consciously aware of at the time. It wasn't something I set out to address, but as often happens when you begin doing deep internal work, what's buried will eventually rise to the surface.

The experience felt a bit like opening Pandora's Box. You really have no idea what might come out. It's unpredictable. Sometimes it's clarity, sometimes it's discomfort, sometimes it's a flood of memories you thought you'd long since moved past. In my case, what emerged was something powerful and incredibly personal—something I now realize had been holding me back for the vast majority of my life. That particular block had kept me in quiet bondage for years, shaping my decisions and dimming my potential in subtle but persistent ways. (That story is one I'll save for another day.)

What struck me most was how much I didn't know was still buried inside me. I'd been so focused on cleaning out the "attic"—the obvious clutter at the top of my mind—that I completely overlooked the "basement." And let me tell you, that basement was brimming with its own stories, memories, and unprocessed emotions just waiting to be dealt with.

Doing this kind of work can be emotionally exhausting, and at times even overwhelming. But it's also deeply liberating. Because once those old blocks begin to clear, you start to feel lighter—not just mentally, but physically, emotionally, and spiritually. It's like removing hidden weights you didn't know you were carrying. And while it can be an intense process, the freedom that follows is more than worth it.

As I continued on this journey of self-discovery and subconscious reprogramming, I couldn't help but wonder just how many generations are unknowingly impacted by beliefs that were never truly *theirs* to begin with. These beliefs—about money, success, relationships, identity, and worth—are so often passed down like heirlooms, wrapped in love and good intention, but rooted in fear, scarcity, or outdated worldviews. And because they're rarely questioned, they get reinforced, generation after generation, until they become invisible frameworks shaping our lives.

I began to notice the subtle but powerful traps we can so easily fall into—ways of thinking and living that feel like our own choices but are, in reality, inherited blueprints we never consented to. What's more, it's often not until we are physically or emotionally removed from the environments and relationships that shaped us that we finally gain the distance needed to *see* the patterns clearly. That's when the shift begins. Perspective is a powerful thing, and separation— whether geographic, emotional, or situational—can be the very thing that cracks the lens wide open.

This became especially clear to me when I discovered that the second major block I released in 2024 was not even something I had directly learned or been taught. It was a deeply ingrained belief that had been circulating in my family for nearly a century—originating from the 1930s. It wasn't something shared with me intentionally. It was more like background music—

always playing, always present, quietly shaping decisions and dynamics for generations. That realization shook me. It reminded me how much of what we carry isn't even *ours*—and yet we live as though it is.

From that point on, my meditation practice deepened significantly. It became less of a wellness habit and more of a mission—an intentional act of seeking. I wasn't just meditating for calm or clarity; I was meditating with purpose, determined to create lasting, meaningful change in my life. And now, I'm committed to helping *you* do the same.

The truth is, while many things in life are beyond our control, the desire for change has the power to unearth action steps we *can* take—actions that can disrupt patterns, shift narratives, and rewrite our internal scripts. But before we can make that shift, we must first do one crucial thing: *decide*. We have to commit to change, not just as a concept, but as a practice. And that practice begins with acknowledgment—with the willingness to examine what's been living inside us, unquestioned, for far too long.

Sometimes the greatest obstacle isn't what's ahead of us, but what's within us—what we haven't yet faced. But once we shine a light on those inner blocks, we reclaim our power. And that's when transformation truly begins.

DO YOU BELIEVE IT BECAUSE IT'S THE TRUTH, OR IS IT THE TRUTH BECAUSE YOU BELIEVE IT?

Whether what I've said here so far fully resonates with you or you're thinking to yourself, *What on Earth is she talking about?* please know that I only teach lived experience; everything I share, I've personally endured. Some of these things don't work for you? That's A-OK! There's absolutely no need to feel compelled to dig into everything I'm sharing if you don't want to. I simply hope that in sharing my journey, I'll help make yours a bit easier—recognizing that no new information one absorbs is greater than his/her emotional state. But I digress...

I had another realization when I discovered this "breakthrough" and subsequent process. When I stumbled upon this information, I was in the midst of a legitimate emotional upheaval. What I was experiencing at the time was the kind of holding-it-in, deep-breathing, *feel-like-I'm-choking* upheaval that demands attention. It wasn't just discomfort—it was an internal alarm sounding loud and clear: *something has to change, and it has to change now.* I knew I couldn't keep going like that. I needed relief. I needed movement. I needed transformation—and I needed it fast. That level of urgency became fuel. Looking back, I genuinely believe it was one of the most significant contributing factors to the success I achieved shortly afterward. I didn't question it; I just surrendered to it.

DO YOU BELIEVE IT BECAUSE IT'S THE TRUTH, OR IS IT THE TRUTH BECAUSE YOU BELIEVE IT?

It wasn't until the previously mentioned conversation—about recording your own affirmations or reprogramming content—that I began to understand something deeper about human motivation. The person I was speaking with seemed skeptical, not just of the method I was sharing, but of the need for it at all. And it hit me: the missing link was *pain*. There was no urgency in their life. No catalyst. No discomfort forcing their hand.

Because the truth is, there is no greater motivation for change than pain. When everything is fine—or even just tolerable—it's easy to put transformation on hold. But when life starts to feel unbearable, when your inner world begins to scream louder than your distractions, *that's* when real change becomes non-negotiable.

Your level of receptiveness, your willingness to take drastic action, is often directly proportional to how deeply you're hurting or how urgently you need a shift. And that's where the disconnect was in our conversation. This individual was comfortable. Curious, maybe—but not uncomfortable enough to take action. Meanwhile, I was drowning in discomfort, grasping for something—*anything*—that could offer relief or direction. So when I found a solution, I didn't just dip a toe in. I dove in headfirst. I went *all in*. I had no choice.

To this day, I suspect that person still wonders whether the steps I took were *too much*. Whether the process was necessary. But here's what they didn't understand: *it was necessary for me.* Because I wasn't trying to tweak my life—I was trying to survive it. The pressure I was under wasn't optional, and neither was the decision to change. It wasn't a nice idea or a casual experiment. It was a lifeline.

And that's why I believe, so strongly, that your pain can become your portal. The discomfort you're feeling isn't here to punish you—it's here to wake you up. To push you toward something better. And when you reach that point where staying the same is more painful than the effort it takes to change, that's when everything begins to shift.

CHAPTER 3

THE QUESTIONS YOU ASK ARE THE PROBLEMS YOU SOLVE

Creating the right frame is everything. It helps you see things in a different light, often impacting your feelings towards the challenge you're facing. Think of a frame as a particular perspective or lens that gives meaning and filters a message or alters an emotion. If you're reading these words, you're likely looking for tools to change and are sick and tired of, well, being sick and tired. If reframing your problem doesn't help you solve it or at least make it more manageable, there comes a point when there's only so much complaining one can do before action is required to solve the problem at hand. Not acting to solve the problem? The pain isn't bad enough.

While that may sound harsh, it's the truth. The first time the head of the networking group I mentioned earlier told me those same words, I was taken back and became defensive. I also told him he didn't understand my pain. His response? "Heather, you are very smart and very capable. You know exactly what you need to do but are just not ready to do it. When you are, this conversation will be in the rearview mirror." He was 100% correct.

The choices we need to make are often not easy, but those same decisions are often the most impactful. If you're feeling emotionally distressed and suffocated in your life, I'd encourage you to consider the questions you're asking—because when you live in an age chock-full of information like we do right now, remaining ignorant is a choice.

What is it that makes the situation you're in undesirable? What is it that makes your life uncomfortable? What is it that you'd like to change? Once you're clear on these answers, the *whys* becomes equally critical to understand. Did you create your limitations? Are external contributing factors in play?

I recognize change isn't something that can happen quickly or easily for many. You may have a family that depends on you—parents, children, or other reasons why sudden change simply isn't an option—but remember that I'm not suggesting anything drastic. Just small, sustainable changes over time. I often say that the advice I share is very much based on the recipient.

Just as life isn't a one-size-fits-all thing, my advice must align with that person's current situation. I wouldn't offer the same advice to a 30-year-old that I'd give someone in their 40s, 50s, 60s, or 70s, for example. We have different commitments at different stages, but regardless of your current circumstance, remember nothing is forever. That much is true. Change is inevitable in life, and it's resistance to the same that amplifies stress.

No matter how frustrated we may get with any type of situation, change does happen—and *will* happen. The question is: How will you control changes set to impact the trajectory of your life? You don't necessarily need to do as I did, though, waking up one morning and saying to yourself, *You know what? To heck with it! I'm moving to Manhattan! I'm going to sell my house because I'm done with all this!* There may also be other actions you can take over time, incrementally, that will change the direction your life is heading in. Whether this is the case or not, just have an intention—and commit to it.

Think about compound interest. A small investment, in time, can yield significant dividends: the power of said change based on time, not the size of the investment. Contributions may in fact be so small they don't make that much difference in your day-to-day life and are probably not even missed. Over time, however, the result becomes significant. The exact same thought process applies here.

As for another analogy, if you sail or enjoy the water as much as I do, you might know that charting a course that's even two degrees off—especially during a long journey—can make all the difference in the world if you hope to make it to your destination. Little things *matter*. Don't neglect the power of small actions and the compounding power incremental changes can make here.

I know intimately how suffocating it can feel when every day feels like a thousand years and every moment feels endless; but if you commit to *knowing,* or at least having an idea of what that destination looks and feels like for you, you'll have something to hold on to. Create a space for said idea to evolve in your mind as you nourish it and begin to envision what that other life looks like—what that *vision* feels like. I remember how when I made the decision to move to Manhattan, I began to visit with more and more frequency and engage in activities that made me FEEL as if it were already home: popping into the city for lunch or dinner and walking around Central Park for hours, imagining an apartment a short walk away. Walking along the streets, I'd imagine what it'd be like if one of the adjacent buildings were my home.

I likewise create images in my mind that my eyes can also "see," finding this a highly effective tool for

manifesting. My goal here isn't to impress my beliefs
upon you but rather share tools I've found particularly
effective. Whether or not you choose to implement
them is entirely up to you, going back to the power of
the subconscious mind and the energy generated by our
actions. For me, little by little things did begin to
change. Once my energy began to shift and I began to
feel the *emotion* of my future, circumstances slowly
shifted into place that allowed me to move forward.
Create the vision, acknowledge your power, gain clarity,
and move forward: knowing that what you seek is
already in you. After all, you would have never been
gifted the dream if you didn't have what it takes to fulfill
it.

In life, two sets of factors impact our experiences:
contributing factors and determining factors. While the
former are typically elements we have zero control over
(e.g., the economy, our job, or our gender or race), we
possess the ability to control the latter. It's less about
what's happening around you and more about how you
allow these same factors to impact you. Will they help
you develop or otherwise trap you in an emotional
prison?

Back when I was a consultant, I found myself frustrated
for a period of time when I didn't believe my
contribution was particularly valued based on my
compensation. Recalling the house story I shared

earlier, a large factor feeding these frustrations were the random expenses hitting my wallet at the same exact time. Suddenly, the same job I was so grateful for when I got it and paid me exactly what I'd asked for—more than I'd ever made before—now had me feeling agitated and frustrated. Why? Because my circumstances had changed, my need for more money, a contributing factor in the growing dissatisfaction with my job. Once I sold my house and no longer had those costs, however, those same frustrations dissipated to a large degree as the expenses disappeared and I was living in the place I'd dreamed of for so long. My determining factor reframed everything.

I often give the following advice to people who are ready to leave their jobs to kickstart a brand-new venture with anger fueling their motivation: if you start working on your dream with funds from your current job, your anger will transform into gratitude because your motivation and goals have changed.

This brings to mind a pitfall so many of us fall into without even realizing it. When you're an employee, a compensation agreement exists based on your time and service—those first months on the job invaluable and precious. Things are as great as they'll ever be, and you're just relieved and appreciative you even have a job in the first place. Then circumstances undoubtedly evolve in your life, creating a financial burden that

causes said job to lose its luster. What's happening in
your own personal life is not the responsibility of your
employer, however. Can you demonstrate how any
additional efforts on your part warrant a raise? Many
people reach a point where they feel entitled and
disgruntled—their pay no longer proportional to their
expenses—but it's the question of *value* that must
always remain top of mind for both employees and
employers.

If you're looking to switch careers or start your own
business, it's critical to understand the problem you're
solving and what you're bringing to the table—ensuring
your question is framed correctly. Far too many people
go into business and then look for people to sell to
rather than understand challenges within a specific
sector and subsequently craft solutions to solve them.
When it comes to a new career, aim to wrap your head
around problems your new company is seeking to solve
and how you're equipped to help with your particular
skillset. Want a significant raise? In this case, my most
meaningful piece of advice is to apply your skillset in an
industry where the same is hard to come by: creating
automatic value as you're not competing with others
who have the same credentials.

For example, my degree in architecture meant seeking a
position with a developer (or someone else in the
building industry) would have made logical sense; but

guess what? With environmental consultants often part of development project teams, my ability to read drawings—thanks to said degree—shined through as an asset most of my colleagues lacked and meant I could capitalize on this same skill within this field instead. Think of it as the chance to seek out "industry-adjacent" opportunities.

Another example? Let's say you're a communications expert hunting for a new job. While you can certainly consider working for a marketing firm—where you'd be a dime a dozen—another option is to seek out a job with a science-based company, working for a pharma or biotech outfit perhaps where your skills are rare and thus create more value. A simple mindset shift here can yield significant dividends.

Allow me to end with this thought. I know people who make an hourly salary of $30, $300, $3,000, and $30,000, each having the exact same 60 minutes to do their work. So, this is the question: What differentiates the person making $30 from one making $30,000? The answer? *Value*. Now, some of you may read this and think to yourselves, *Why on Earth would anyone pay $30,000 an hour for anything?* To that, I'd respond that what if in that hour, you learn how to make $300,000 in 30 days guaranteed or your money back? In this case, that $30,000 is a bargain! The questions you ask are the problems you solve. Seek to provide value by finding the

solutions your audience or employer would feel foolish
not to pay you for—whatever the price.

CHAPTER 4

BUILDING CREDIBILITY WITHOUT CREDENTIALS

It's a pervasive problem. As desperate as you may be to break into a brand-new industry, you hold back: assuming you don't have the formal credentials necessary to do so. Sound familiar? If so, let me assure you that if you have any sort of experience and/or knowledge at all, you have what it takes to pursue the goal, the dream, the desire, and the vision you have for your life. Now, I understand we live in a society that's highly competitive and chock-full of people who've achieved remarkable things. *You* rank among them though, with experiences worth taking the time to document and share. This, my friend, will give you all the credibility you need.

If you've been following me, you know I've used this same tactic throughout my entrepreneurial journey: taking the time to write books (four of them now) and then shift into new industries I don't have formal credentials in, putting my knowledge out there so that anyone desirous of collaboration can understand my thought process, skillset, capability, and (most importantly) passion. For those of you not necessarily familiar with my story and meeting me for the first time, allow me a moment to share a little bit of my background...

Back in 1995, I came to New York from Grenada to study and earn my bachelor's in architecture—following this up with a master's in environmental technology. During my architectural thesis, the jury failed to appreciate the project I'd chosen for my thesis (proposing the renovation of a historic site in my home country) as they didn't think it was appropriate to alter such a storied structure. This failure, however, essentially changed the trajectory of my life. I was forced to retake the previous semester with a new project that was safe, ugly (quite frankly), and lacking any sort of passion so I could simply *pass*. I'd hardly call that final project a vision, but it was indeed *final*: marking the beginning of the end of my desire to be an architect. Completing that horror depleted me of my love of design, and my distress was quite visible in this new iteration especially because I only had five months left on my visa and was thus forced to make up the failed semester during the summer so I could graduate.

When I had finally finished everything necessary to earn my architectural degree, I had zero desire to be an architect anymore—I was *done*. Taking to heart a comment made about my "environmental insensitivity," I went on to pursue my master's in environmental technology and become an environmental consultant. I remained in that space for 15 years.

If I'm going to be completely candid, I should mention that from the day I walked into that firm—even though it was a great place with great people—I felt like a misfit, believing I lacked the natural aptitude my colleagues had as this job wasn't my original goal. It wasn't my vision. I'd ended up in an industry I hadn't set out to enter simply because I needed a career at the time and had a degree that was completely useless to me; so from almost day one, I knew this wasn't something I'd do for the rest of my life. Talk about things not coming naturally! It was just not my natural habitat, and I knew it, as simply a skill I'd acquired. So, I did what I had to do while knowing another chapter would be necessary as environmental consulting would most certainly not the be-all and end-all to my story.

Approximately one year later, a friend of mine—also from Grenada—who worked with an alcohol distributor asked me to help her with spirit and wine tastings for her Long Island accounts (where I lived at the time). I thoroughly enjoyed it! I'd teach people about spirits and wine and didn't even mind doing so after waking up early for my primary job. On some days, I'd get up at around five or six o'clock in the morning, work my day job until late afternoon, and then perform a tasting at 6 pm. It didn't matter how long my day was or how far I had to drive; I always had the energy for my side hustle, as if I'd just woken up and started my day, and paid attention to that feeling because I genuinely loved it.

I eventually got to thinking about what my life could look like if I worked in the alcohol space on a full-time basis and subsequently sought out opportunities to do so. Unfortunately, no distributor would hire me. Why? Because my resume read like one of a scientist. Seeing my degrees, they assumed someone with a bachelor's in architecture and master's in environmental technology couldn't possibly know anything about selling alcohol. The word "overqualified" was thrown around a lot at the time.

By this point, I'd been doing tastings for maybe two or three years with accounts requesting me by name thanks to my work ethic: the same one I employed as an environmental consultant and now carried over into my work as a promotion model. I showed up on time. I stayed the entire length of the tasting. I engaged with the customer. I did all the things I was supposed to do to the tune of really good results, which stores appreciated. I never had any issues booking jobs as a brand ambassador and made great money while doing so—a huge bonus! Of course, I wanted more of where that came from, but as I said: people often judge us based on our "credentials," not knowing our knowledge. If we don't take the time to share our experience, they'll certainly never know what we're capable of.

I eventually decided to launch my first company, All The Tastes of New York, after feeling like I just needed an *out*—a stepping stone into the world of alcohol I just couldn't seem to break into. All The Tastes of New York, in its infancy, was a company created around experiential dining. The concept? Rather than sit down to eat an entire meal at one restaurant, diners would enjoy an appetizer at one location, their entree at a second, and dessert at a third. My amazing relationships with various wine and spirit brand representatives paid off here, giving me the means to offer tastings and pairings at these venues.

As time passed and years went by, my parallel career played out over nine years'. It was like a running joke; when people asked me what I did, I'd say, "Well, that depends. There's Heather by day, an environmental consultant, and Heather by night: a brand ambassador." It became clear, though, that the time had arrived to focus on life after environmental consulting. When I finally pulled the trigger in spring 2014—two years after starting my company. I realized very quickly that my business would have a difficult time growing without any real marketing budget for one primary reason: no one knew I existed. With the benefit of hindsight, I can say with confidence that the number-one challenge facing any small business struggling to win customers isn't related to subpar service but instead likely the result of people not knowing said service exists in the first place.

As you think about what you'd like to do and the dream you'd like to pursue moving forward, answer this key question: How will you fund it? I encourage you to hold on to your job for as long as you possibly can before fully embracing entrepreneurship so you can work out the monetary kinks in the process. You don't know what you don't know, and many times—especially in the beginning before you gain clarity, you'll likely make a lot of expensive mistakes, a primary reason why so many young businesses die in infancy. If you're not well funded (and even if you are!), correcting costly errors can easily become emotionally overwhelming and stunt your growth. It's inevitable as you assume you lack necessary resources and thus hesitate to correct yet another mistake while hoping for the best; no longer making decisions for the company to grow, you're instead afraid of failing and not making necessary changes while consuming your operational budget.

The ins and outs of brand-building of course involve much more than just money. After I stepped out on my own to give my full attention to my business, I received a LinkedIn message from someone who'd started a publishing company and was looking for new authors.

had no intention of writing a book at the time. Deeming this information irrelevant, I essentially filed away the opportunity in the recesses of my mind.

Three months later and trying to build my brand, I was hired for Astoria's Restaurant Week and decided to engage with local distillers, brewers, and vineyards. Coming face to face with a plethora of New York State brands, it occurred to me that I had no idea New York had such a thriving alcohol industry. Having had my ear to the street as a brand ambassador doing tastings for major brands over the previous 10 years, I was shocked I hadn't realized so many craft distillers existed in New York—the realization that if I had no idea, many others also likely didn't either, which sparked my recollection of the previously mentioned LinkedIn message. I decided to reach out.

Sure enough, the person who'd contacted me was still looking for authors. I suggested an idea: "How about I write about craft spirits in New York?" Turns out she didn't have anyone writing in that genre and thought it was a great opportunity. I signed the contract on October 7, 2014 and recorded my first interview for *Discovering the New York Craft Spirits Boom* 13 days later. The book debuted at Book Expo America on May 25, 2015. Talk about an aggressive schedule! I didn't have a clue but did think of my great aunt who always said, "When ignorance is bliss, knowledge is folly." I had no idea what I'd agreed to; all I knew was that I needed to get it done and trusted myself to do so.

Realize something: I'd never written anything in my life up until this point and didn't consider myself an author or writer of any kind. I realized, though, that in order for me to score the publicity I needed, this was the path of least resistance and an economically sound one at that. The investment in time, however, was absolutely brutal. Talk about a grind! Nevertheless, I knew success in this arena would give me credentials I didn't otherwise have in the space as people would get to know me while I added "author" to my name. Perhaps this sounds completely insane—and it was! There's no sugar coating it, but I'd jumped on an opportunity and wasn't about to blow it simply due to a time crunch.

Allow me to share my logic and how I decided to get this done with zero experience as a writer. Given my greenness, I needed to figure out the easiest approach and decided to pursue an interview-style book where I'd simply share the stories of other people and thus remove the pressure of creating actual content: seeing myself as a vessel used to convey the stories of these individuals while benefitting from doing so. I ultimately interviewed 30 distillers throughout New York State, located everywhere from Brooklyn to the Finger Lakes, and based my book on the same.

With each interview, I told the story, I shared the brands, and I took the pictures. I also decided to include cocktail recipes since I'm a human who loves cocktails and creating experiences (which is precisely what All The Tastes of New York did at that point). Thinking methodically and logically, I sought to share and include this content in a way that people would find fun and engaging while providing locations where they could buy and experience distiller products whether liquor stores, bars, or restaurants. I covered all bases, providing the distiller and consumer with a book that was actually an experience in itself.

There was a method to the madness, though; not only were 30 included distillers motivated for the book to sell, but six different establishments where readers could engage with the product were as well (happy to oblige when I approached them about selling the book on site). This goodwill-type approach is a great option, I believe, for new writers concerned they don't have enough to say just yet but are in fact serving and touching multiple people while doing something universally good for everyone as a rising tide. Before understanding how to help yourself, think about how you can help others: the number-one aspect of aligning with the purpose you're seeking. The first path to purpose is service, and you'll automatically serve yourself by default after serving others.

Book signings followed, including a particularly memorable one in Albany. I'd made it a practice to always do book signings in towns boasting a featured distiller and inviting them to attend, once again creating experiences in novel ways (no pun intended). On this particular day, the distiller shared he was desirous of finding salespeople in New York City—a place where they were struggling to get placement. At that point I realized: *Hey! I have the skillset to do this.* Although I'd started in environmental consulting as a scientist, I eventually segued into business development and thus had legitimate business development skills, experience, and knowledge just waiting to be applied in the alcohol space with this man set to benefit.

This calls to mind a huge tip: most knowledge is transferable. Let that sink in for a minute. Too many people miss out on opportunities because they view their knowledge in a very linear way and thus stay within the confines of the same industry. Think back through your experience, though: How can you transfer what you know across industries? It goes back to the primary reason those distributors never hired me, not understanding what an environmental consultant could possibly know about alcohol sales. Beyond just selling alcohol, though, I'd be selling *intellect* but as part of a defined process: making appointments, employing a system to document my contacts, and doing meaningful follow up. These are all transferable skills, and I knew I possessed what it took to adapt my knowledge.

This is also how All The Tastes of New York wound up shifting from an experiential dining company to one focused on supporting New York State craft distillers; I knew that if one distiller was experiencing the previously mentioned problem in NYC, they were all. Once I became clear on the service I needed to provide—getting products into Manhattan bars and restaurants, something every brand the world over is desirous of—I contacted other distillers in the book. Those were very easy yeses, as I'd already provided evidence of my desire to share their story and do what was necessary to work with their best interest in mind, so they trusted me with their products.

After about two years spent selling New York State spirits, I began to receive a lot of interest from international and domestic brands thanks to a little thing called Google; in typing "New York State spirits" into that magical little box, online searchers would stumble upon my book *Discovering the New York Craft Spirits Boom*. That brings me to another very important point: SEO (search engine optimization) is nothing short of essential for any business endeavor, but be sure to do your due diligence in this respect. After all, you are who Google says you are; so when people look you up, whatever populates on the page is what they'll believe. In thinking about branding, remember your company is essentially based on your personal brand so be sure to pay attention to this (something I share a lot).

Whatever you name your company as a solo entrepreneur, I strongly suggest you make sure it's "Googleable" and create meaningful content to share— so when people search for you, you can control the narrative and help them find you. Gone are the days of being a ghost online, assuming the space is only for celebrities or "big" names and thus not bothering. Guess what? You're now competing with the people who *do* bother. Think about it. When you look for a doctor online, do you go with the one who has 500 reviews or none? I'll go ahead and guess the former and that you likely interpret a lack of information with a lack of quality. Please store this advice in the front of your memory for easy retrieval down the road.

Getting back to branding, though, All The Tastes of New York ultimately evolved into Tastes Brands after I started working with clients from other locales. I couldn't have international and domestic products in a portfolio named after New York State products, after all. My portfolio began to shift organically, with my price point shifting significantly as well. Even though the needs of these clients mirrored those of New York brands, I could charge considerably more as they were funded very differently as new market entrants: allowing my business to grow since I could now afford to hire good salespeople, only possible thanks to clients with greater resources.

This brings me to the story of Tastes Brands and the reason why I wrote my second book, *Before the Glass: Things To Consider When Entering The Booze Business*. Keep in mind I was a small business owner with a small team of salespeople and a small tasting team: a distributor-agnostic operation given that many of these brands were suffering amongst distributor portfolios, none getting the attention they needed. Our service, in turn, provided the sales support they needed to land on shelves and cocktail menus in bars and restaurants. Because of our small size and that we were quite literally a "boots on the street" service, we couldn't carry many products—typically no more than six brands, especially given that each brand had multiple products. Add to that the concrete jungle of New York City dictating walking and taking public transportation everywhere, the grind was brutal while toting a wine bag with up to 12 bottles.

I was therefore very intentional with the products we took on, none of which could compete with each other meaning brands needed enough distinction for us to do our job well. I'd typically select products for our portfolio at the beginning of the year given the transition period, knowing (quite honestly) most brands didn't understand the gestation period and lag time between presenting a product and accounts actually making a purchase. Product testing to ensure consumer interest, meanwhile, called for tastings. It was an expensive undertaking, these unknown labels competing with mega brands that required a fraction of the work to sell.

Onboarding one particular brand back in January 2018 and going over our contract, I discovered a problem: he'd in fact done every single thing I'd told him *not* to do when we'd met months earlier in October. It was clear: working with this brand would ruin my reputation, which is not something I was willing to do. It's for this same reason that I never had to solicit a brand, every single client referred to me as I'd always do right by my clients and accounts. Knowing nothing was worth ruining any relationship for any reason, I decided to walk away from that client and keep my reputation intact—to the detriment of my finances. So angry and upset, I decided to write *Before The Glass* on the heels of this experience and did so in one weekend, knowing I literally could not afford to have that happen ever again.

Neither my services nor my salespeople were inexpensive by any means, so beginning the year without that client in my portfolio meant I was starting 2018 with a loss: a hard lesson in knowing your right-fit client and setting expectations accordingly. In my defense, we had gone over the general terms months before and I had no way of knowing he'd have an emotional meltdown prompting him to import two pallets of product set to triple the cost of what we'd initially agree to take on.

In Before The Glass, I took time to explain how the New York market is different than any other these brands may be accustomed to and outlined strategies I used to place product—explaining just how expensive the process was and laying out related costs. I also included the general gestation period prior to breaking even or seeing results, the logic being that for a couple of dollars, you could go buy this book on Amazon and (should you take to the contents) forge a partnership with no issue. In this way, how I do business is clear up front to avoid unproductive, unhappy, and unprofitable relationships.

Depending on who your client is, this particular book-writing strategy is often very lucrative as you won't waste time on the wrong people and the right ones will find you. Once you're clear on the problem you're solving and the composition of your audience, message clarity comes into play as part of a solid formula for growth. So many individuals, when they go into business, believe they can be everything to everyone— but this is simply not true and instead a surefire strategy to fail. You must be as clear as you possibly can regarding your model customer so they (your "ideal customer") can find you. Know who that person is. Now, I understand that when you're starting out you may have no idea and thus eventually need to shift to a new target; but do your best to pinpoint the person you're looking to serve with as much clarity as you possibly can, making it that much more likely said person will find you. I myself have needed to shift on many occasions and know that as a small business, "niching" down can feel scary; but you don't want to waste time on clients who aren't a good fit, both of you lost as you end up spending time and resources in the wrong place.

If you recognize a need to shift, *shift*. I'm not saying don't make decisions that drift from your vision but instead that you should practice having conversations geared toward solving a particular problem. If you end up solving other problems inadvertently, great! Either which way, practicing how to connect with your ideal customer and solve their problems is key. The questions you ask are the problems you solve, so work to understand their pain and pressure points and what keeps them up at night to tailor your services per these specific needs. Rather than find customers for your business, find specific problems you're uniquely qualified to solve knowing many others struggle with the same. It's after this that you can create content (i.e., a book or videos) sharing your knowledge on the topic so that clients searching for a solution can find you.

As for my own clients, they unfortunately lost half their revenue stream quite literally overnight when COVID hit. If I'm being completely honest, though, I'd already reached a point where consulting felt like a better fit as

I'd realized so many of the brands I represented were making a lot of very expensive mistakes—finding me at what was essentially the end of the product line with no options to make any real difference at that point. I thought to myself: *If I can connect with brands earlier on in their journey, I can help prevent or at least mitigate the expensive mistakes they're making to help keep them in business.* It was in fact the fate of many brands who essentially treated their business like guesswork without fully understanding the industry they occupied. This is one reason I stress gaining as much clarity as you can regarding your ideal customer and how you can best serve them; in understanding their pressure points, you'll remain one step ahead.

If I'm being completely transparent, I'd known for a while—deep in my gut—that I no longer wanted to be in the alcohol space, not even as a consultant. This same truth, once fully acknowledged, was both freeing and terrifying. For years, I'd carved out a unique identity within that industry and knew the language, the players, the pace, the strategy. I knew how to make brands shine. I'd spent an entire chapter of my life immersed in that world, and truthfully, it had given me a platform as the springboard that taught me branding, positioning, and how to build a name for myself in a competitive market; but what happens when the very thing that helped you rise no longer *fits*?

When the opportunity presented itself to become a content creator, it didn't feel like a detour—it felt like a lifeline. It was as though all the marketing, storytelling, and branding wisdom I'd accumulated over the years had finally found a new container, a new purpose. I fully embraced the shift and began to thrive, pouring myself into my work while creating campaigns for lifestyle brands primarily focused on beauty and the home. Stepping into a new dimension of creativity as both the architect and the messenger and helping to market other people's visions, I was shaping my own voice in the process.

But here's the thing about evolution—it never really ends.

After almost three years of producing content, collaborating with brands, and growing my digital presence, I began to feel something stirring again. A quiet discomfort. A restlessness that had become all too familiar over the years. I've come to understand this is often how transformation announces itself—not with chaos or dramatic upheaval but with a soft and persistent whisper that says, *This isn't quite it*. When that whisper becomes loud enough, it's impossible to ignore.

That gnawing feeling returned, the sense that while I was indeed headed in the right direction, I still wasn't quite *there*. I was adjacent to my purpose and orbiting around it but not yet centered within it. There was a deeper calling, something more aligned with the impact I wanted to make that could only be answered by stepping outside of what was comfortable and familiar—again.

That's when I decided to write *Pivot: Because Life Doesn't Always Go As Planned.*

I realized I was being called, once again, to share my truth but while using my voice to help others navigate their own turning points this time around. Writing *Pivot* felt like a line in the sand, marking the end of one season and the beginning of another. I knew instinctively it wouldn't be just a book but indeed the cornerstone of my next rebrand.

Now, let me pause here and say this: the word *rebrand* is often misunderstood. People tend to associate it with superficial changes—new colors, a new logo, maybe a catchy tagline—but the type of rebrand I'm talking about is far more personal. It's about internal alignment. It's about letting go of old titles and roles that no longer reflect who you're becoming. It's about having the courage to shed skin in front of the world, knowing full well that some people will be confused, some may lose interest, and others may fall away entirely but doing it anyway because staying still feels like dying a slow death.

Writing *Pivot* helped me reclaim my voice as a guide and mirror for others navigating uncertainty. It gave me permission to own all the iterations of myself—the environmental consultant, the brand strategist, the spirits expert, the content creator—and fuse them into something more expansive honoring not just what I *do* but *why* I do it.

It's funny how life works. You think the previous chapter was your big break and your ultimate path before life lovingly disrupts you once again—not to punish you but to position you. That's what *Pivot* represented for me as both a personal testimony and a professional bridge, allowing me to step into a new space of service rooted in transformation, storytelling, and strategic clarity. I share all of this not just to narrate my own evolution but to make something clear: you are allowed to change. You are allowed to outgrow your former goals. You are allowed to leave behind the things that no longer bring you joy, even if they once did and paid the bills and you worked really, really hard to get there. Growth is not betrayal. It's *becoming*. The moment you stop giving yourself permission to evolve is the moment you stop living. If there's anything I want you to take from my journey, it's that reinvention is not a detour—it's the path. Every pivot, every redirection, every internal tug is part of your unfolding. Trust it.

So, when I felt the pull of yet another rebrand, I didn't resist nor try to force myself to love a version of life that no longer fed my spirit. Instead, I chose to listen. I chose to create. I chose to use my story not as a script to be followed but as a spark for others feeling lost at their own crossroads. Subsequent feedback I received surprised me, readers sharing their struggles to pivot and embrace change as I simultaneously changed the trajectory of my own life once again. *Create Your Own Table* naturally followed, opening my eyes to how so many people out there were getting stuck—not for lack of knowledge but rather insufficient courage, clarity, and confidence, the lack of a starting point greater still.

As my own purpose and the reason I was put on this Earth came into focus more and more, a familiar saying played on a loop in my head: "We are most qualified to support the person we used to be." Think about that for a second. Think about what you've gone through, challenges you've overcome, problems you've solved, and how you came out on the other side; other individuals have experienced the same and are thus ripe for your knowledge and guidance. Because we so often fail to see our experience as valuable, we fail to share it. It's a tragedy, really, given so many people out there who've experienced the same hardship or challenge but haven't received support for fear of shame—suffering in silence and believing they're all alone.

In beginning to realize this, I decided to step back and assess the emotions I experienced while enduring periods of fear, frustration, embarrassment, and not feeling like I was *enough*. We so often miss out on teaching opportunities, thinking that in order to teach you must have the "credentials" to do so—when really all you need is to overcome the struggle yourself, not even being that far ahead but simply *ahead*. The closer you are to whatever problem it is that you've solved, in fact, the more relatable you'll seem to the people you're supporting: not so far out of their league that they feel uncomfortable nor too far removed from feelings of embarrassment or shame or anything else keeping them from getting the help they need by connecting with you. If you're closer to them and the problem, the solution doesn't seem as unattainable (in contrast to, say, people we idolize while believing we'll never get where they are because they're seemingly so far ahead).

Think about it. You've read the books, taken the courses, and attended the seminars and events while listening to this God-like person yet fail to take any action on what you've learned. Why? Because you don't see the correlation nor anything in common between yourself and this individual who's apparently so far ahead of you as far as you're concerned. Not only are you missing out on the opportunity of the message and the power of transformation, but you're comparing yourself to that person—not seeing yourself in that light and thus not sharing your own light to guide someone else.

I saw these circumstances with complete clarity after *Pivot* was released, understanding I could help others overcome challenges quite simply because I'd done the same. At that point, my path became clear. Whatever it is you're desirous of, break off bite-sized pieces of the steps necessary to get there so it feels real and achievable. As you become more comfortable and begin to do more in this space while becoming more confident, you will evolve: not failing to act due to a mindset grounded in *leaps* rather than *steps*. It's about taking the first step of the journey, not getting to the top of the mountain. Absorb the stories I'm sharing in bite-sized pieces, likewise, so you can implement them per what's comfy and palatable for *you*.

Now that we've talked about content a little bit, let's discuss the second hurdle to writing a book: publishing. Fortunately, we live in an amazing age where platforms like Amazon exist to take the middleman out of this process: getting your product to market sooner, efficiently, and much less expensively than ever before. You can of course use a traditional publisher if you prefer but will have a timeline entirely dictated by them in doing so—if they're even interested in publishing your book in the first place. Nevertheless, publishers can help with editing, printing, sales, and marketing, which is desirable for many people.

When I wrote my first book, I felt fortunate to have a publisher especially since I was a newbie to the process. I also assumed that was really the only way to get a book to market at the time. Working with a very, very, small team—essentially just the publisher and a couple assistants—I went on to experience a painfully time-consuming process, possibly due to the fact it was a boutique publishing company but rough nonetheless. Editing alongside my editor and self-marketing my book, I of course did what was necessary but ultimately had zero control with everything going to the publisher. Though I actually didn't see one single penny from that book—just a ton of printing costs every time I needed copies—the business it generated was huge so I cannot complain.

Having endured that experience, there was no going back after Amazon came along and gave me full control over the process. The hands-on experience I'd gained with my previous publisher meant I understood what needed to be done, while freelance platforms like Fiverr helped make the process that much more seamless. *Before the Glass* was a very, very short book (remember how I said I wrote it over the course of a weekend?) but thankfully 100 pages long to meet the Amazon publishing requirement as part of an easy intro to self-publishing. Once I got to those hundred pages, you better believe I was done after saying what I needed to say. On the other hand, Amazon eBooks have no size limit—certainly something to keep in mind if you'd like to test out the process.

I believe I used a stock image for my cover, and my brother helped me with the graphics. Although Amazon did offer print on demand, I wound up going with a local printer in New York City that gave me an amazing price to print maybe a hundred copies I'd take to industry events rather than source them from Amazon. That was a personal choice, as was my decision to fully rely on the support of Fiverr for *Pivot*: using this freelancing platform as a resource to find my editor, graphic designer, and videographer for my marketing video. There is no shortage of freelancing sites just like this one where you can source individuals who perform myriad tasks.

I'd also suggest creating your own "publishing company." Nothing to be nervous about, let me assure you! All I did was list the name of my company, Doltam Creative Solutions, as the publisher on record. The corresponding reason? Doing so allows traditional bookstores (e.g., Barnes and Noble) to sell your book. For me, it simply meant putting my company name in that space and using it when I bought my barcode (scanned to find the price). You can do the same if you'd like!

I decided to create an audio book for *Pivot* as well and made the decision to record in a professional studio. You can also record and upload your own audio as another option, but the idea of doing that quite frankly makes me twitch. I personally consume most of the books I read on Audible, so the idea of offering my book in audio format made a lot of sense. After all, consuming books in this way when you're on the go—whether you're taking public transportation or driving—is a wonderful way to multitask. So, I wanted to give anyone consuming my content that option.

Another important consideration when thinking about the value of writing a book is the press release, particularly if your goal in doing so is to get your name out there. Press releases are sent out to news wires, the cost of which is dictated by the author depending on how much geographic territory you want to cover. You can either stay local within your state (less expensive) or include neighboring counties or even states (more expensive), knowing it's completely up to you based on your audience. Investing in a press release is particularly valuable for branding, as news wires will offer up your story by default to media outlets hungry for news and things to share: information their listeners and readers may be interested in, going back once again to searchability. If someone types your name or book title into Google, the press release will come up containing whatever information you and your PR company decide to share. It all goes back to controlling the narrative, determining what to put out there to tell your story and how you'll show up in the world. Just like taking the time to write a book will give you the credentials need to build credibility in your chosen market, taking the time to send a press release will improve your online presence and position you as an authority in your space.

Last but certainly not least are book signings. While traditional venues like bookstores, libraries, churches, and community centers are always solid choices, I personally love the energy of book fairs and street festivals. These events may not require a big financial investment, but they do require your time, preparation, and presence. And they are *so* worth it.

Book fairs not only give you the chance to position yourself as an authority in your subject matter, but they also allow you to sow seeds—one conversation, one signed book, one heartfelt exchange at a time. There's something powerful about showing up and being seen in real time, engaging with people who are genuinely interested in your story or message.

What I especially enjoy about book fairs is the chance to connect with fellow authors. It's always fascinating to hear about their creative process, their journey into publishing, and the lessons they've learned along the way. You never know when a chance meeting might lead to a meaningful collaboration or a new friend who truly understands the writer's road. Sometimes your genres or industries may even align in ways that open new doors. Speaking about collaboration, don't forget the book signing in Albany, New York that I mentioned earlier where the distiller was present. That event changed the trajectory of my business and life. The value of that one-on-one interaction can spark tremendous ideas and should never be discounted.

Another important benefit? Content creation. Attending a book fair is a fantastic opportunity to gather high-impact visuals and stories that support your brand. I once hired a photographer for a fair I participated in, and they captured incredible shots of me signing books, speaking with readers, and sharing insights about my work. Those images became invaluable assets for my website, blog, and social media channels. There's something powerful about seeing someone *in action*— t tells a much stronger story than simply talking about what you've done.

So take the time. Do the work. Show up fully. If you're reading this, I already know you're committed to differentiating yourself, gaining clarity around your message, identifying your ideal audience, and discovering how best to serve them.

Keep these core pillars in mind—they are the very legs you'll need to build a table strong enough to hold the vision you're bringing to life.

CHAPTER 5

CREATE YOUR PERSONAL BRAND

Let's dig into the concept of a "personal brand," something that essentially identifies all of who you are authentically. In doing so, first think about why people typically reach out to and connect with you. Do they need help with a particular thing or in a particular area? What exactly is that area, subject matter, or topic, that thing you do so naturally? Your personal brand is inherently *you* and effortless as the essence of who you are and your natural embodiment, the very foundation you're built on. I often like to say to "get in alignment with your assignment," your goal in this stage of life is to think about how you'd like to evolve personally and/or as an entrepreneur. Let's think about the elements of your table just as the book title says, knowing the key element of any business is one's personal brand at the core.

If you're transitioning into a new professional phase, the corresponding process will organically play out in one of two ways. Obviously, I have no idea about the thoughts swirling around in your mind or what your vision for your life looks like, but for sake of simplicity, let's consider two likely circumstances:

1) You're desirous of creating a business based on what you currently do in your "day job" and your genuine expertise.
2) You're shifting careers—stepping out of corporate and into a new space or perhaps close to retirement—but with a considerable amount of information to share and (quite frankly) a need for money, not wanting to be employed by someone else doing something you're not interested in.

Whether you want to continue in the general industry you're in and serve others independently through your own company or otherwise pursue something completely new but without formal credentials, building your personal brand is a critical step that will serve you in both: bringing clarity to yourself and others regarding your expertise.

Based on what I shared in the previous chapter, there's no need to worry about formal credentials since writing a book gives you all the credibility you need as a "resume" for people unsure of how you fit in a particular industry. Want to go out on your own? Your book gives you the wherewithal to do so. With the support of a company no longer behind you, taking the time to write a book also provides a reference point others can refer to: giving them a sense of who you are independent of your previous company. Many people in fact overlook this.

This calls to mind an experience I recently had with someone who'd been employed by the same company for well over 30 years and never expected to be let go. As a matter of fact, this person had expected a note of congratulations for bringing in a huge project when she was summoned to the office manager's office on one particular day—only to be (you guessed it) fired. It's truly a gut-wrenching story as this individual had spent her life focusing on everything the company needed, never taking the time to create any kind of online presence outside of the job so what little information was available revolved entirely around said company. It's important to never reach that level of comfort, although many would call this dedication, where you don't know where the job ends and you begin, a tried-and-true formula for disaster particularly later on. The most difficult part of the story? I shared this same insight with her—someone I'd known well over 15 years—to be told "I'm too busy" anytime the subject of even a proper LinkedIn profile came up. Now, of course, it's not like we're working for free, right? I get it. You work, get paid, want the raise, and are busy climbing the corporate ladder; but how tragic is it to realize you'd leaned your ladder against the wrong wall when you finally reach the top of it?

This further speaks to the importance of controlling one's narrative online, knowing anyone in business needs clients to build said business. You are who Google says you are: harsh, but true. Fail to take the time to share your knowledge and who *you* are independent of any company you're employed by or affiliated with and you'll do yourself a huge disservice down the road.

Really process what I'm sharing here. Let's use 15 years as an example, a relatable period of time after which many employees find themselves in management or seeking executive-level jobs elsewhere. Now responsible for bringing in new business, you meet with a potential client who looks you up and finds nothing: zip, zero, zilch beyond the story of you with a different company. Alternatively, perhaps you decided to go out on your own and likewise need clients. Looking you up to the tune of negative results, a prospective client has no sense of who you are because you're a ghost on the Internet. None of us are immune to this, so take the time to create an online presence: not some sort of digital junk or Instagram posts about your weekend shenanigans but instead content about your genuine knowledge and interest in a particular subject. Simply showing you're a well-rounded person outside of your company's platform can pay dividends. I'm a huge proponent of personal websites in particular, the alpha and the omega and my number-one piece of advice especially for my clients.

When I was an environmental consultant back in 2007, I transitioned from my work as a scientist to business development: my job at that point to build our pipeline and thus connect with attorneys, industrial clients, and real estate developers, essentially any business potentially in the market for our service. This involved making tons of warm and cold calls in an effort to set up appointments, and it occurred to me just how much time I was spending googling different companies and key decision makers to learn their general background and assess a potential fit. Just as I was taking the time to find them online, it stood to reason they'd likewise take the time to verify who I was. Wanting to control the narrative, I put the information out there I wanted them to find: presenting myself in the way I wanted to be received while making it easy for them to find me in the first place.

Not enough people, quite honestly, think like this. Back in those days when building a website wasn't the turnkey process it is today and legitimate coding was required, I was fortunate enough to have a younger brother with this particular skill set and so asked for a favor: a simple one-page site, www.heatherdolland.com

(no longer active for reasons I'll share momentarily), so that when I called to request an appointment or left a message and contacts went online to google me, they could quickly and easily find what I wanted them to know with no need for a frustrating search. As for the site's contents? A succinct bio relaying my role as the business development manager at XYZ company and a bit about myself. I'd actually gone to the CEO at the time to explain my logic and request "approval" for my website to be linked to the company's, receiving his blessing in return.

I remembered getting a lot of flack from my colleagues for doing this, many of them asking why I was making so much effort for the company. Little did they realize that in doing so, I was actually making my own life easier; the more appointments I secured, the easier life became for me. There was something else, though, as the quality content I was creating eventually served me tremendously when I stepped out on my own. While the information on my website of course changed at the time, I had zero issue ranking on Google as the site had been established 7 years prior.

So yes, there's power in using your name as a website domain as it leverages SEO (search engine optimization) with no need for anything fancy: just a simple one pager, your picture, and general information about who you are and what you do. You can also create a blog—an area on your site where you write posts on various topics of interest as thoughtful content—if you're feeling a little bit more assertive and want to go one step further. , your website will give future clients or employers a sense of who you are. Assuming you picked up this book because you're eager to start your own business, you know you can't have a business if you don't have clients. Make it easy for them to find you! Beyond bringing more of them on board, you'll avoid the chance they'll google your name and come up empty and thus risking your credibility. No matter what your business is, do this first and include valuable information on your website with time to rise up the ranks on Google so that when the time comes—even months or years from now—you've done yourself a favor when it comes to prospective clients.

Not too long after I got my own site up and running, LinkedIn became more and more popular, and I began to speak about the importance of taking the time to create meaningful online presence with my colleagues. The key word here is *meaningful*. If you're a professional, take time to create a LinkedIn profile at the bare minimum—which makes everybody's life easier. When I'd call to make an appointment and then share which of my colleagues would be in attendance, for example, it made life so much easier for everyone if said colleague(s) had taken the time to create a proper profile—a lighter lift to secure the appointment given this established baseline.

Let's get back to understanding your personal brand, specifically. In doing so, avoid becoming so overwhelmed by any notion that you must remain committed to whatever it is you decide to share in the early days. Take me, for example; by this point, you guys know my story and that I've evolved numerous times both professionally and personally in my life. Your start by no means dictates your end, and what's important is that you create a meaningful presence: making sure what you're putting out there isn't junk and will ultimately give the people who find you—whether a year from now or 5, 10, or 15 years down the road—some context about the person they'll want to do business with. As I mentioned earlier when it comes to having proper online presence, if content is king, *context* is queen.

Allow me to pause and share something of importance for those who've changed their name due to marriage or otherwise. In this case, you cannot simply update your name on your existing website and must instead create a brand-new domain name; it's for this reason www.heatherdolland.com became www.heatherdollandtamam.com. Check it out! I share all of who I am here with absolutely no shortage of information for those trying to get a sense of me. Also knowing clarity is king in business, I went ahead and created a second (more targeted) site— www.doltam.com—sharing one message with one audience to give my clients a place to find what they're looking for without the need to search. Now, I'm not saying you need to create and maintain two websites; I'm just sharing what *I* did to create the space I needed to present all of who I am online.

With regard to social media, it's smart to leverage platforms like LinkedIn that have powerful algorithms to help you to rank higher on Google (LinkedIn also recently introduced a video feed that mimics Instagram reels and YouTube shorts). As far as YouTube is concerned, the platform's robust algorithms make it a powerful search engine in itself just like its parent company Google. Videos created on YouTube have their own independent links on Google, and if you use all of these platforms in a cohesive way, they'll do an amazing job to help build your personal brand. So, is one better than the others? If I had to narrow down the list, I'd name YouTube as king due to its search capabilities—calling up responses to questions just like Google and with the power of video to boot. When you're creating content—no matter the topic, business, or problem you solve—be sure to align the subject matter of said video or post with the pressure point of the searcher. What would this person likely type into Google or YouTube when searching for a solution to the problem he or she is facing? It all goes back to the power of search engine optimization.

As for social media content, I'll again reiterate to not create junk while understanding the time commitment required to do so. It's huge! Having done this for a very long time now, however, I can say with full disclosure that I didn't properly .everage YouTube until recently and eventually realized what a colossal mistake that was. Given my work as a content creator, the brands I worked with zeroed in on Instagram or TikTok—the former by far the preferred platform—so I focused my energies there. As I shifted into this space and my messaging changed, however, I realized Instagram wasn't suitable for long-format messaging and thus preferred YouTube and LinkedIn given my desire to connect with professionals, business owners, and would-be entrepreneurs: shifting my thought process and attention based on where my audience was.

This brings up another crucial point: the importance of having a clear understanding of your ideal customer or audience. Creating content with this party in mind—and delivering it where they're most likely to engage—maximizes both your time and impact. To work efficiently myself, for example, I now focus primarily on creating wide-format (horizontal) videos for YouTube and then take this single piece of content to reformat videos into vertical versions for the other major platforms: an approach allowing me to do the work once and repurpose it strategically across multiple channels.

Although platforms like TikTok now support videos up to 10 minutes long, I personally prefer to create shorter clips from a longer video. For example, let's say you film a 25-minute video that walks viewers through the full process involved when baking a cake from start to finish. You can upload this full video to YouTube and then break it down into five separate 5-minute clips, each focusing on a specific step in the process, and share these shorter videos throughout the week on other platforms (e.g., Instagram, Facebook, and LinkedIn).

If you decide to use this approach, be sure to shoot the original, longer video in horizontal format and center *yourself* in the frame. This is important because when you crop the video into vertical format later on, you'll find most apps will automatically trim the sides and only retain what's in the middle of the screen. By positioning yourself correctly from the get-go, your content will stay visually balanced and professional-looking across all platforms as part of a strategy allowing you to extend the reach of your content and save hours of time by repurposing a single video in multiple ways. Remember: work smarter, not harder. For the sake of clarification, while it *is* possible to reformat a horizontal (wide) video into a vertical (narrow) one, the reverse isn't true—meaning you can't stretch a narrow-format video into a wide one without compromising quality or composition. So, always start with wide-format to enjoy the most flexibility while repurposing your content later on.

When it comes to creating valuable content, understand your customer's pain point(s). Why does that person need you? Your goal in creating and sharing content is to address the same. Not about jumping through hoops to find your right-fit clients, it's about them finding you organically once they realize your messaging aligns with their struggles and challenges: knowing and feeling you understand where they're coming from as you've created content meant for *them* (rather than creating a business and then finding people who "fit"). My recommendation is to think about your ideal client and discern the problem(s) he or she is facing, demonstrating you understand this and offering up a solution accordingly so prospects know you have the answers they're seeking.

A final—and incredibly powerful—aspect of building your personal brand is, of course, networking and collaborating. While these two pillars are often overlooked or treated as afterthoughts, they're truly where the magic happens. Once you begin to gain clarity on your voice and the value you bring to the table, building relationships becomes not only easier but much more aligned. Should you decide to write a book—especially one connected to your story, mission, and/or area of expertise—networking becomes an organic next step in expanding your visibility and positioning yourself as a thought leader.

Think about it: a book is so much more than a product to buy from a shelf or download from an app. It's a conversation starter. It's a gateway. It's a platform that allows you to curate experiences, host discussions, lead workshops, and build communities around the subject matter you care about most. It creates a reason for people to invite you into spaces, whether digital or physical, as an anchor for collaboration with other experts and entrepreneurs in your field. Beyond just saying "I have something to offer," you're showing the same, page by page, with clarity and authority as an author.

When I published *Discovering the New York Craft Spirits Boom,* the actual book became an experience in and of itself. Readers used it as a guide to discover distillers throughout New York State and planned weekends around such excursions. Likewise I was invited to a number of spirits festivals and industry events to do book signings. All of the natural exposure surrounding those experiences made my evolution into the alcohol business an organic one, setting me up for a business I'd never even intended back when it all began (you may recall how I'd written the book to promote my experiential dining business but then saw an opportunity for a business to be born while at an Albany, NY book signing with a featured distiller).

When I published *Pivot: Because Life Doesn't Always Go As Planned*, then, I didn't just think about the book— I thought about the *doors* it could open and used it as a springboard to create content and online talks and support people I knew I could help. Those experiences were built around transformation, career shifts, and owning your voice; people showed up not only because of what I had to say but because of what the book represented, a clear message and call to action. That, my friends, is the power of authorship.

Book signings, podcast interviews, speaking engagements, panel discussions, and brand collaborations are just a few of the doors that open when you position your book as more than a product but as *proof* of your expertise and vision. Authorship signals you're serious about your message and committed to serving a specific audience, creating instant credibility even with total strangers. Most importantly, authorship is a *superpower*, a badge of commitment and symbol of leadership. Too many entrepreneurs overlook this, assuming it takes too much time or that they're simply not "ready." What I've learned—and continue to see—though is that writing a book isn't just about the finished product but about who you become in the process and what you unlock afterward.

The truth is, your book can go further than you can. It can travel into rooms and reach people you haven't met. It can open doors while you sleep. It can advocate for your brand, your mission, and your value—before you ever even walk in the room. You just need to be bold enough to put it into the world.

When you pair authorship with strategic networking, creating meaningful content and collaboration, the power of your personal brand will be unmatched. You're only limited by your imagination and your willingness to show up—and believe me, the world is waiting for you to do just *that*.

CHAPTER 6
YOUR VISION

When it comes to your vision, my first bit of advice is to not let your destination become your limitation. What does this mean, exactly? When I started my first business, I did so because I essentially needed an outlet (as previously mentioned)—knowing where I was wasn't where I wanted to be. Unable to get hired in the field I yearned to explore, I needed to create a space of peace and solace for myself while also knowing I desired a certain amount of geographic freedom. Travel was important to me, particularly as a person born in Grenada and with family scattered quite literally all over the world. I wanted the freedom to live and explore as much as my heart genuinely desired yet also recognized a problem: my vision and the business I'd created were in direct conflict with each other as my physical presence was required for events, experiences, and (most important) sales. After all, I couldn't sell product to a liquor store or restaurant without being physically there.

While that was *my* specific challenge (more on that in a bit), others may find their knowledge base unable to support their vision—which is precisely when I'd urge you to seek out education. This can in fact come in a multitude of forms. For example, when I entered the content creation and voiceover space, YouTube was my teacher; I absolutely attended YouTube University all day, every day. There's nothing wrong with realizing you must dedicate the time necessary to piece together the education you need to support the vision you have for your life, especially true if you're looking to shift industries and start a new business in an area you don't have formal credentials or any sort of knowledge in. You must work on the foundation you'll ultimately build your new company on.

When I launched All The Tastes of New York, I'd always had a passion for food and wine (which is obviously why I chose that particular business). Prior to this though and while trying to figure out what on Earth I could do with my life that would make me happy, I considered becoming a chef—especially because I'd always been an avid cook. I decided to sign up for a certification course at the French Culinary Institute in Manhattan, an hour commute into the city twice a week as I'd lived on Long Island at the time. Beyond the time commitment, it was by no means an inexpensive endeavor; yet I knew it was my future and that I needed to do something different to get to the next place. About two weeks into the six-week program, however, I realized that in absolutely no world would I actually become a chef. Between the heat of the kitchen and long hours spent on one's feet—I'd already suffered from chronic back pain—I was like, *Okay, this isn't happening, but I'm happy to have had this experience and learning opportunity.*

I didn't look at it as a waste of money or time—gaining knowledge never is—and while it was tempting to feel that way, I acknowledged I'd learned valuable information. The most valuable? A career as a chef was not in the cards for me. Perhaps you're saying to yourself, *Well, Heather, you didn't have to spend a couple thousand dollars to learn that.* You know what, though? I'll always put my best foot forward when trying to carve out the very best life for myself. Was it a bit of an expensive lesson? Sure, but it provided absolute clarity that whatever visions I'd had of life in a kitchen cr restaurant were simply not going to happen. With that, I knew I needed to shift and pursue something different.

The following year, I thought about my love of food and wine and considered that while the food part hadn't worked out so well career-wise, maybe the wine part would. I thus decided to take a vinification course with the American Sommelier Association—essentially a wine foundation course—yet again very quickly I realized the life of sommelier was not for me. These people, or "somms," as they're better known, legitimately live and breathe wine and have a passion for it in a way I simply did not. Ever watched one of those documentaries about winemaking? If so, you know just how grueling the process is and why individuals with this particular skillset are paid so handsomely. It could have been a beautifully elegant path—especially as a New Yorker surrounded by no shortage of high-end Michelin Star restaurants—but in my soul, regardless of my love of beauty and elegance, I knew this wasn't it. With zero need to convince myself that anything else was the truth, I'd learned valuable information in the process and looked onward: satisfied and confident that fundamental knowledge I had in both industries was enough to start All The Tastes of New York. It's not like I was going in cold following my work as an environmental consultant, and I was excited to create a business around creating food and wine experiences.

Now, back to what I said previously about my vision of having the freedom to travel despite my work as a business owner. In trying to wrap my head around this concept, I realized I needed to learn more about entrepreneurship in the hopes I could eventually get to this point. I *also* realized that sometimes we don't know what we don't know and thus decided to seek out coaching, buying my first coaching program back in 2012. It was a six-week program designed for people who ran online businesses, and I remember thinking how it wasn't an exact match nor speaking to exactly where I was at that moment; yet I knew that if I paid attention and invested in this course, because it was very much an investment, I'd gain the tools necessary to see my ultimate future vision through.

Fast forward six years later when All the Tastes of New York evolved into Tastes Brands with the focus on supporting distillers and spirit brands. I decided to hire a business coach since I was having issues scaling and knew I'd done as much as I could with the knowledge I had but needed to go a step further with the help of someone else. Think back to what I shared in the previous chapter about building your personal brand, about making sure you're sending the right message so the people who need you will recognize and connect with said message while knowing you're for them. With this in mind, allow me to share how I likewise forged a connection with this particular coach and knew she was the right one for me...

I was about to go walk my dog, about to head out to Central Park when I glanced at my laptop and saw an ad pop up on Facebook. Looking closer, the message this person was sharing stopped me in my tracks. *Are you a business owner? Have you done ABC? Have you gotten to point XYZ, after doing this, this, and this? Feel like you've hit a plateau and can't scale?* It was as if this woman was in my head. Beyond my head, it's like she'd tapped my phone and heard me vent these same frustrations to whoever was willing to listen, intimately aware of every single challenge I was experiencing. In that moment, I immediately identified her as my right-fit person. The irony? I hadn't even been looking for her, honestly not knowing at that point that I needed to hire a coach. I didn't even know such a thing even existed as the answer to my problems, stuck and not knowing what to do. Then, all of a sudden this person comes along who's sharing ALL of these pressure points I'm having. *Thank God!* It was the solution I needed, a person with the answer to the question when I didn't even know how to frame said question in the first place.

That coaching package was by far the largest investment I'd made in myself up to that point, knowing my business would fail in short order if I didn't go out on a limb and try it. After everything I'd put in to make it work, I needed to feel satisfied that I was doing everything in my power to keep my business afloat and would know I'd at least given it my all if it failed despite the investment. It indeed proved to be the best investment I'd ever made within a couple weeks, however, and what's jaw dropping is that her fee—which seemed astronomical at the time—ended up mirroring what I charged my own clients with zero issue.

It's the perfect example of what I mean when referring to clarity in messaging and creating a meaningful online presence. If you take the time to create meaningful content, the people who are seeking you will find you;

and given the improved efficiency of online algorithms nowadays, this process works even better now than it did back then let me assure you. Your first responsibility, though, is to make sure you create meaningful content (worth repeating multiple times throughout this book, if you've caught on to that by now).

As time evolved and I continued toiling away at my business, it remained (frankly) not in alignment with my ultimate vision: to be able to travel with ease, running a business not tied to one particular place. Tastes Brands, on the other hand, still required I be present in New York City selling and doing all the things I needed to do to support my clients. When 2019 wound up being a year filled with challenging clients (and even more challenging staff experiences), I made the decision to shift gears and focus on consulting—knowing the knowledge I'd accumulated over the years would prove invaluable. I thus entered 2020 with a handful of clients, fully intending to use this as a transition year before COVID came along in March. After I lost my clients and accounts to maintain, I used my time to consult while having no idea when the shutdown would end (a number of distillers produced hand sanitizer from spirits as a way to supplement lost revenue during this time). I consulted with a handful of companies for a few months—some industry adjacent, others new products interested in entering the New York market—but in my heart knew that was the end of that. The end of Tastes Brands had come, and I was ok with it.

A short three months later, I stumbled into the world of content creation having finally figured out a way to enjoy a bit more freedom while acknowledging the irony in that there wasn't so much of it to go around at the time (COVID and all). Yet, I'd finally found a way to align my work with my knowledge and skillset while making money from home—chasing the sun around my apartment to shoot videos with optimal natural light. Then as I shared earlier, things shifted yet again three years later when I realized I needed *more* and so wrote *Pivot: Because Life Doesn't Always Go As Planned*. This brings me to where I am with you now: living completely in my purpose, using my wide swath of experiences to serve. More importantly, I'm nice and comfy online and thus have the means to touch you all globally. Where I am right now reflects the vision I'd sought during a 13-year journey, not wasting anything in all that time. I share this knowing it's very frustrating to feel like you can't see the end of the road, knowing you're heading in the right direction but uncertain of the destination. There's nothing wrong with that nor anything wasted. In viewing every experience as a steppingstone, it's that much easier to push through and embrace it.

What you're doing throughout this period is giving yourself the opportunity to witness yourself, allowing yourself the chance to reframe your challenges and problems and how to solve them. Perhaps this involves a brick-and-mortar business, a bakery or restaurant maybe. Knowing all of our needs are different, my recommendation is to merely think through the vision you have for your life and realize that learning process— that path—isn't always straight. It will likely contain a certain number of "failures" along the way, but I encourage you to embrace these knowing there's no success without failure. Success would most certainly not be what it is if failure didn't exist, in which case everything would remain as the status quo, right?

The long and the short of it is that I'd have no business at all without all the failures, struggles, and challenges that helped get me here. I'd also be completely useless to you without them, my greatest periods of growth occurring when things went completely awry. My skillsets were molded during periods of adversity requiring me to exercise muscles I frankly didn't even know I had, most notably my extraordinarily strong ability to get back up. I very much see failure as part of the journey—just part of the course—and focus on overcoming, which I know and I trust. Once you begin to trust in your ability to get up, falling down just becomes part of the process. As I like to say, "If you fall on your face and see where you're falling, you'll never fall there again" and "If you fall on your back, if you can look up, that means you can get up." Don't focus on falling. It's your belief in your ability to get back up, that minimizes the fall. Focus on the recovery and rebound. That's the secret sauce.

You can also think about "failure" in terms of tests or experiments. Say you're in a lab on a quest to create something. In this case, first-time failures are by no means a thing; after all, no one is pulling your funding because your very first test didn't produce the results you were after. Quite the opposite, in fact. Most companies know it takes years to create a stable formulation for anything as a completely accepted fact, so why in the lab of life, then, is failure so taboo? When something doesn't work, you change, adjust, and try something different—rinse and repeat until you finally find success.

With this in mind, I'd strongly suggest reframing your narrative while understanding the importance of experience with no greater teacher than mistakes; these "failures" indeed make you so much stronger as a professional and more valuable to your clients with a proper number of them under your belt. It's in this way that you become relatable thanks to real-life experience and the school of hard knocks. What you share, in turn, isn't based on something you read in a book or saw in a video but instead grounded in your own trials and tribulations. If a client comes to you, he or she is likely doing so with a problem that needs solving. Had you never endured your own challenges with none of your own failures to speak of, guess what? You'd be absolutely useless as a problem solver.

In working to clarify and then act upon your vision, embrace your problems and failures: viewing them as topics for content you'll discuss on your website or share in videos you'll create on YouTube to the benefit of those who find you. Those very challenges are truly your lead magnets, so wrap your arms around every single one of them knowing you're only as strong as the problems you solve along the way.

CHAPTER 7

YOUR PURPOSE

We all have a unique "soul message" typically created and defined based on the life we've lived, experiences we've overcome, and/or traumas we may have witnessed. Your purpose, likewise, is something that is very much inherently *you* and the core of who you are. When you work within your purpose, it won't even feel like work because you're doing the very thing that nourishes your soul: feeding the passion that is your authentic self and creating in a way that's uniquely you.

When I think about working in my own purpose, I think about my journey: coming to New York as an architectural student all those years ago and now supporting those ready to step into entrepreneurship as their natural, authentic selves. It seems like such a far cry from where I began. How on Earth does one evolve from a person who left her home country to go halfway around the world in search of degrees and credentials only to end up here?

What you guys may not realize is that I'd always get in trouble at school as a child (something my parents most certainly can attest to), feeding into my story. "Heather speaks too much in class" was a common refrain written at the bottom of my report card year in and year out, my parents never particularly fond of receiving this news. Fast forward to 2007, then, when I transitioned from my role as a scientist to business development and thought to myself, *Well, look at that. Now I'm quite literally getting paid to talk.* When I ran into my old high school principal a couple months later during a visit to Grenada and shared the news with her, she enjoyed a proper chuckle. It was true, though! The very thing that had gotten me into trouble as a child wound up serving me well as an adult.

I was recently reminded of an experience I had when I was 18 years old—two years after graduating high school in 1993—and was asked to serve as the master of ceremonies for the graduating class of 1995. I had no idea what my principal (the same one just mentioned!) saw in me back then to believe I was capable of taking on such a gargantuan task but smiled at her doing so when I came across the letter she'd written thereafter to thank me. The biggest irony of this reminder? I'd spent a tremendous amount of money honing my speaking and writing skills at age 48 whereas 18-year-old me had stepped onto that stage and truly commanded it with no particular talent other than a lack of fear.

I also remember being the queen of the side hustle back in those days with an affinity for learning new things. It was the early nineties, all about box braids and hair extensions in my world, and I can recall learning how to execute these—always a quick study—and then testing myself. My friends would then ask me to do the same for them, probably the very first side hustle I ever engaged in: hair, nails, eyebrows, you name it. Looking back, I can see my natural persona as a perennial communicator who's enjoyed helping people ever since I was a child. By the same token, getting older meant becoming a "proper" adult and earning a "proper" degree to give me "proper" credentials. Many of us in fact do all of these things so that society will "accept" us and see us in a particular way, yet I find it fascinating how I've pretty much ended up essentially exactly where I began: nurturing my love of speaking to people while creating meaningful connections and making a difference.

Provided the chance to share my knowledge with others, I'll happily do that. It genuinely doesn't feel like work to me, and while I did all the "things" and checked all the boxes, I eventually found it necessary to check my *own*. Isn't it interesting (and, quite frankly, sad) how we feel inclined to live our lives based on other people's definition of success? I guess I had to go through all of that, though, to reach the point where I finally accepted that wasn't for me. Unfortunately, so many others remain stuck in place forever because the idea of doing something different—despite their desperation and feelings of misery—is absolutely terrifying.

If you can personally relate to this same notion, please know I'm here for you. I also have a question: Have you ever stopped to ask yourself, *Who creates these boxes we're all so busy checking anyway?* What was their motivation, and why are we so willing to oblige? When you begin to realize how restrictive they truly are, you likewise begin to realize our traditional education system was designed for a very different age than the one we live in. Now, don't get me wrong—I am pro education and not an antiestablishment person by any stretch of the imagination. I very much consider myself an online educator in fact, so please don't misinterpret what I'm about to say. The reality of our education system, though, is that many of these institutions were established during the Industrial Age when people needed to operate machines as part of a workforce qualified to perform specific functions. Back then, people were fed the necessary information to go out and do the jobs they were assigned in a permission-based society where strict conformity ruled the day.

In contrast, consider our current era: one filled with technology and AI, beyond anything the Industrial Age established. Our timelines have collapsed—calling for much different skill sets—and to even think of a world when Google didn't exist feels like we're talking about the Dark Ages. Back then, you didn't need an online profile or presence. It simply wasn't a thing, but it very much is now. So, zooming out, I genuinely believe the wider world must acknowledge the newfound skills we now need to be competitive. Even as I sit here and write this book, I'm in fact speaking it thanks to the power of transcription: using an app that translates speech to text as a much different experience than my previous book-writing experiences. Though many edits are of course required, I can create an original manuscript with much greater speed and efficiency than I did even 10 years ago while writing *Discovering the New York Crafts Spirits Boom*. That was a painfully slow experience I'm afraid, but no more; the volume of content I can now record in a few days' time mimics weeks of work when I was writing my first book. No exaggeration!

Moving along now, as you begin to think about your purpose and how you can best show up in this world as your authentic self, my recommendation to consider all of the things that speak naturally to who you are. This brings to mind my architectural thesis jury back in 1999. While I touched on this earlier, I didn't mention a related development that's happened since. Recall how I'd chosen a historic Grenadian site for my architectural thesis, one of the oldest structures in the world in fact.

Not believing I had any right to touch this, the thesis jury failed me—wanting nothing to do with my proposal to renovate the site and also adding a museum and restaurant and restoring the fort to its former glory. How dare I attempt to renovate such a structure! This, of course, changed the trajectory of my life, and I shared this same story in *Pivot* (released in July 2023). Two months later, my father sent me an article from a Grenadian newspaper announcing World Bank plans to fund the revitalization and renovation of Fort George, quite literally the very same thing I'd proposed in my thesis in 1999. As I write this, the work continues.

The bottom line is that the people around you may not understand the vision you were given. In my case and as part of my unfortunate experience, the powers that be decided to fail me, label me, and make me question myself. To be completely honest, that same failure followed me for longer than I realized—taking up residence in my soul and becoming embedded in my subconscious mind. It also became part of my identity in a way I hadn't realized at the time, the weight I'd carried for 23 years lifted only after my father shared that fateful news out of my home country in 2023. Funny enough, I was 23 years old when the incident had gone down back in 1999—go figure!

I came to realize I wasn't working in the industry I'd loved for so long due to that "failure," one that not only had me questioning my judgment at the time but my professor questioning hers as well—the failure a mark against both of us with sentiments that we'd both exercised poor judgment. I longed to pick up the phone when I finally received that redemptive news and say, "Michelle, there was nothing wrong with us. We just had a vision the thesis jury didn't and were ahead of our time, every single aspect of our vision now being realized." Even as I'm sharing this, I strongly recall the feeling of confusion we'd both experienced because we genuinely couldn't wrap our heads around the failure. We were forward-thinking in that moment; the gatekeepers, however, were not. We are ahead of the room we were in.

To add further context, my thesis professor was the first person to build a legal "shipping container home" in New York City: a Williamsburg, Brooklyn apartment building made from (yes) four shipping containers. Michele Bertomen was very much a visionary and trailblazer who, like me, thought so far outside the box she didn't know where the box even was. To say we had a lot in common was an understatement—we even shared the same birthday! Her passing in 2013 meant she'd never know our dream for Fort George had indeed come to fruition, a victory I so wish I could have shared with her.

You probably have your own version of this story, one in which some sort of decision maker neither agreed with nor supposed your vision. I've indeed met a number of individuals in the aftermath of this experience whose futures were stunted by the advice or direction of a teacher or authority figure who failed to see or share in their vision. Lacking enough sense of self to realize these are merely others' opinions, they found it difficult if not impossible to grow as individuals. The challenge with these experiences when we're younger is that we believe the people in power must be right, automatically making us wrong and giving us no choice but to accept it.

As for myself and for the sake of transparency, at 23 years of age I no longer believed I had what it took to be an architect—deeming my classmates smarter than I was while trying to achieve a goal I didn't have the capacity to fulfill. I thus pursued my master's in environmental technology as that same thesis jury had labeled me as "environmentally insensitive" (as previously mentioned), assuming I didn't have any choice in the matter since I would surely fail as an architect. I honestly believed that. As you all know by now, though, my story is not one of woe, and I've gone on to enjoy an amazing life—the benefit of hindsight providing clarity as to why the first 15 years of my career were filled with so much dissatisfaction as I sought to find a purpose that would fill my soul.

A thought has stirred within me, though, one that surfaced while I was giving a talk honoring the extraordinary visionary who was Michele Bertomen. For

23 years, I carried the weight of failure, defending the decision of the thesis jury that denied me. I'd convinced myself they were right, that our vision to restore a historic site in disrepair was naïve. Unrealistic. Too ambitious. I buried the part of me that once believed it was possible and silenced the voice that saw value in what others had dismissed. Even now as I write these words, they feel heavy with regret. Because why *wouldn't* you want to breathe life back into something that still holds meaning? Why wouldn't you try to save something worth saving?

I'd stopped asking those questions, though, no longer trusting my own vision and instead deciding to drink the Kool-Aid while absorbing the beliefs of people who couldn't see what we saw: blindly accepting someone else's truth and making it my own while killing my dream in the process. Just like the tragic historical event in Guyana when 918 people followed a leader without question and perished, this was a less-tragic version of the same.

Michele never drank the Kool-Aid. She dreamed boldly, taught fearlessly, and lived with vision. She believed in possibility and in *me*, even when I didn't believe in myself. I never got to tell her what her faith in me meant nor share this full-circle moment, but in a very real way, her legacy lives on in the work I do, the people I help, and the very mission of Doltam Creative Solutions.

That moment of failure—the one I carried like a scar—
became the spark for everything I've built since. Now, I
think of all the people who've lost sight of their own
dreams because they were talked out of them and
instead chose to follow the voice of someone else who
couldn't see what they saw. My work is to help these
same people reclaim that vision while unlearning the
lies, trusting themselves again, and rebuilding—
beautifully.

CHAPTER 8

YOUR TITLE ISN'T YOUR IDENTITY

Knowing we're all in different places and stages in life, I recognize you have your own unique reason(s) for picking up this book. Allow me to take a moment to speak directly to those of you who aren't necessarily interested in building a large business but rather a side hustle: something to generate some money but not necessarily a livelihood. Perhaps you're between jobs or recently experienced a job loss and want to start exploring something you enjoy. If you're not sure where to start, this chapter is for you.

Unfortunately, a job loss (should this be the case) can leave you feeling as if your identity was left behind along with said position. While I mentioned witnessing this experience happen to a friend in a previous chapter, I'd now like to provide some tools that dig a little deeper should the unexpected occur or you're otherwise simply ready to embark on a slightly different journey than the one you're currently on.

I've always believed in celebrating who we are—not in a passive, fleeting way but with intention and consistency. Living your best life isn't about chasing perfection or checking off society's boxes. It's about alignment. It's about being deliberate in how you honor your truth every single day. While "living your best life" may look different for each of us, one thing remains the same: it should never be an afterthought. It's a decision—a conscious, unapologetic declaration that your life, your time, and your joy matter.

This mindset has served as my own personal compass. Whatever I commit to, I do with energy and presence. I show up and show out—not for applause but because I've promised myself I'll fully engage in anything I say yes to. Why? Because my happiness is my personal responsibility. It's not something I outsource or wait for others to hand me. It's the fuel that drives my decisions, my boundaries, and the way I move through the world. learned early on that no one will prioritize my fulfillment the way I will: a simple truth that changed everything. This is exactly why I knew deep down my environmental consulting work couldn't be my forever (though I did find aspects of it fulfilling). I was good at it—but being good at something doesn't mean it's your purpose. A quiet but constant tug at my spirit reminded me I was meant for more: more impact, more creativity, more alignment.

If you're at a crossroads, or even just feeling the itch to do something different, start exploring the things that bring you genuine joy—not what you're obligated to do nor what others expect of you but the things that fill you with peace, energize your spirit, and make time disappear when you're engaged with them. These are often the breadcrumbs that lead to your purpose. Pay attention to what lights you up. Is it something your friends always compliment you on? Something you do naturally even when you're not paid to do so? That's not coincidence—that's clarity in disguise. Nurture it. Explore it without pressure or expectation. Cultivating that part of yourself builds a foundation that will support you no matter what life throws your way.

Also remember that purpose isn't always found in a grand, dramatic moment. Sometimes, it reveals itself in the quiet consistency of what brings you peace. When change inevitably comes—as it always does—your purpose will keep you anchored by something far more powerful than a job title and give you a sense of identity rooted in authenticity, not circumstances. It's entirely possible that the thing you enjoy doing—your hobby, your creative outlet, that thing that makes you feel alive—can indeed generate income. Even if it just produces a few dollars here and there, it's perhaps worth exploring how to formalize the same by creating an LLC (Limited Liability Company) in the name of your passion. Whether you're crocheting, making artisanal jams, painting teacups, baking, designing digital templates, or offering coaching sessions, the point isn't about some sort of multimillion-dollar business idea but rather giving your creativity a container to grow in while protecting yourself in the process.

Now, I'm fully aware that not every passion is meant to become a business. I'm also aware that not every side hustle brings in enough money to feel "worth" formalizing. Here's some perspective, though: life is unpredictable. Smart planning isn't about reacting to crisis but instead creating options before you need them. Even if your passion project feels small or informal, establishing an LLC can position you to pivot with more ease later on should the unexpected happen. I can already hear the pushback; *Heather, it's just a fun thing I do on the side and barely makes any money. Why would I pay to form an LLC?* That's a fair question, and let me be clear: everything I share here is simply a recommendation, not a requirement. You are by no means obliged to take every piece of advice I give, my goal simply to plant seeds that might benefit you in the future especially during times of transition. As with everything I share in this book, I'm speaking from experience having navigated unexpected career shifts while leaning on the structure I built around my passions to support me. These insights come from my journey. My hope? I can help you prepare for *yours* in sharing them.

That said, before you make any decisions—particularly those involving taxes, liability, or business structure—I strongly encourage you to consult with a tax professional or attorney. Everyone's financial and legal situation is different, and it's important to receive guidance specific to your own unique circumstances.

As for the previously mentioned LLC, the primary idea behind this is that if you live in the United States for example, and are a woman and/or belong to a minority group, corresponding programs are available to provide you with support as a small business. At the time of this writing, one of the biggest LLC prerequisites relates to how long ago your business was established versus how much money it's made; so don't overemphasize a potential lack of revenue and brush off this step because it feels too formal. At the end of the day, this is your life—as well as the lives of the individuals who depend on you and surround you. No matter the idea, even just something hanging out in the recesses of your mind, know that pursuing and maintaining an LLC is not that expensive an endeavor. I promise you it is indeed a very manageable thing, especially if you're doing this while having a full-time job as well.

Let me offer a bit of insight, especially for those who might be thinking, *My side hustle doesn't bring in much income. Why would I go through the hassle—or spend the money—to set up an LLC?* I hear this a lot, and I get it. On the surface, it may seem unnecessary to invest in a formal business structure when the money you're earning feels minimal. Here's the reality, though: protecting oneself financially isn't just for people making six or seven figures and in fact even more important if you're not!

Let's walk through a hypothetical. Imagine you've built something substantial—a side business that's brought in $100,000 or even $500,000 over time, for example. Now imagine someone decides to take legal action against you, maybe out of pettiness or misunderstanding, and wins a judgment. It stings, but because you've earned a solid amount, even if you lose half of it, you still have something left to pay your bills and maintain your lifestyle. Now imagine the same situation with a much smaller income, say $5,000 earned from your passion project. If a similar lawsuit were to occur and you're not legally protected, this entire amount could be wiped out with devastating consequences if you're relying on the money to cover rent, groceries, and/or bills. The difference here isn't just about dollar amounts—it's about *impact*.

This is why I believe legal and financial protection is for everyone, not just the wealthy. If anything, those of us who aren't swimming in surplus must be even more diligent. Every dollar matters. Every cent counts. Setting up an LLC is one way to create a protective boundary, safeguarding your personal finances by separating your business liability from your personal liability so if someone ever *does* go after your business, your home, your savings, and your personal bank account are less at risk. It's a layer of protection that's especially crucial when your margins are slim and every dollar is spoken for. So no, forming an LLC isn't about how *much* money you're making—it's about protecting what you have. Whether $500 or $500,000, you deserve to keep what you've earned as a powerful act of self-respect and smart planning while preserving your progress no matter how small it may seem.

Now, let's think a few steps ahead. Once you've registered your company as an LLC, the next important step is to apply for an EIN (Employer Identification Number) that's essentially your business's version of a Social Security number. Issued by the IRS, it's required to conduct various business activities (e.g., filing taxes, opening a business bank account, and verifying your company on social media and e-commerce platforms). Take TikTok, for example. If you're selling products—whether T-shirts, candles, lip gloss, or handmade crafts—and want to direct your followers to your website or online shop, you'll need to upgrade your TikTok profile to a business account. Here's the catch, though: in order to verify a business account, TikTok requires you to submit your EIN (something you can't procure without first establishing your business legally, most commonly through an LLC).

See how all the pieces fit together?

Even if you're operating your side hustle from your kitchen, garage, or living room couch, you step into business territory the very second you decide to sell to the public. Want to grow, build credibility, and eventually scale? These foundational steps are non-negotiable. Setting up these "small" but essential things—your LLC, EIN, and business account—may not feel urgent right now, especially if your side hustle is still small or just getting going, but it's how you lay the groundwork for long-term success with something solid to fall back on in preparation for life's unexpected curveballs. Also remember that doing things the right way from the beginning can also open the door to valuable tax benefits such as business deductions on supplies, software, marketing expenses, and even portions of your home if you're using it as an office.

Now, let me pause here to say: I am not a CPA, attorney, or tax expert. What I am, though, is someone who's been through this process more than once and learned—sometimes the hard way—how important it is to do things correctly from the start. I always recommend speaking with a licensed accountant or tax advisor to fully understand your responsibilities and potential financial benefits. Everyone's situation is different, and the right guidance can save you a lot of time, money, and stress in the long run. In short, don't underestimate the value of getting the business basics in place. It's not just about selling—it's about setting yourself up for sustainability, protection, and peace of mind.

You'll also want to invest in a reliable invoicing or accounting software; it might not feel like the most exciting part of starting your own venture, but trust me, it's one of the most important. If you're bringing in any form of income, whether from digital products, physical goods, consulting services, or anything in between, you'll need a system in place to send invoices, track payments, and manage your finances. Beyond organization, it's about *ownership*. Let me put it plainly: no money, no business. Period. You can have the best idea in the world, the most beautiful branding, and a passion that runs deep—but if you're not getting paid, you're not running a business but instead engaging in a very expensive hobby. You've worked too hard, invested too much, and come too far to not get compensated for the value you bring.

Having the right tools to facilitate payment helps you look professional and credible. It sends a message that you take what you do seriously—and encourages others to do the same! Whether you use QuickBooks, Wave, FreshBooks, HoneyBook, or another platform, what matters is that you have a way to keep track of every dollar coming in and going out. This also makes tax season a whole lot easier and gives you a clear picture of your business's financial health year-round; and let's be honest—nothing kills momentum like chasing

125

payments or scrambling to find receipts. So do yourself a favor: take the time to get your money systems in order. Getting paid isn't just a goal but indeed your right as a business owner, and you deserve to build something that not only fulfills you creatively and purposefully but also supports you financially.

Finally, my last recommendation brings us back to a central theme that runs throughout this book. *You need a website.* I know, I know—I've practically pounded this point into your brain by now. That's because it matters. A lot. Even if it's just a simple, one-page site with your name, your photo, and a short description of what you do, *having your own digital home base is essential.* At the very least, it should tell people what you offer, why you do it, and—most importantly—how they can get in touch with you. You can also use it to receive payments or embed links to your calendar, online store, or downloadable offers. Not ready to build an elaborate site? That's okay! Just start somewhere. A clean, simple page can work wonders.

Beyond the nuts and bolts, there's something deeper here. One of the things I love most about having your own website is that it gives your audience—and potential clients—a place to land. It gives your brand a sense of legitimacy, even if you're still finding your footing, and says, "I take what I do seriously and have a space for us to connect." That simple foundation builds trust, signals professionalism, and allows you to control the experience rather than rely on the unpredictability of third-party platforms.

Because let's be honest—depending solely on social media is risky. We've all seen what happens when those platforms suddenly change their algorithms, shut down temporarily, or crack down on content. Remember when TikTok went offline for a while and creators were scrambling, calling themselves "TikTok refugees"? It was a wake-up call. Many realized they'd built their businesses entirely on rented land—platforms they don't own and have zero control over—and here's the kicker: on social media, all it takes is one person reporting your account to lock you out with no warning nor any real recourse. Your visibility, your content, and even your customer base—gone in an instant. That can't happen with your website, which belongs to *you*. Your name, your narrative, your rules.

Think of your website as your digital storefront. Whether you're a full-time entrepreneur or someone dipping your toes into a new venture, it offers stability and credibility. It also gives you room to grow—adding new services, products, blog posts, testimonials, or whatever else supports your journey. So don't wait until everything's "perfect." Done is better than perfect. Start with a simple page. Claim your domain name. Plant your flag. Because if there's one thing I've learned, it's that *having a space of your own isn't a luxury—it's a necessity.*

127

Thankfully, many super easy, plug-and-play platforms exist for website-creation purposes, allowing you to enter your information quickly and easily. Once your site is ready, you'll want to pair it with a nice professional email address and then work on building your email list—another huge benefit of having your own platform.

Platforms like Wix, Squarespace, Weebly, and GoDaddy Website Builder offer intuitive drag-and-drop templates where you simply add your images, text, and branding elements. WordPress (especially with an Elementor or Divi theme) is also a great choice for those seeking a more robust, customizable option with built-in blogging and e-commerce features, though with a slightly steeper learning curve. Planning to sell digital or physical products? Shopify is an excellent all-in-one solution for this.

Once your website is live, you'll want to take a few additional steps to position yourself as a professional. The first is setting up a branded email address that matches your domain—hello@yourname.com or info@yourbrand.com, for example—as a small detail that makes a *huge* difference in how you're perceived by communicating credibility and professionalism while telling people you're serious about what you do. Sending emails from a Gmail or Yahoo account just doesn't have the same weight when you're building a brand, trust me.

The next important step—and one of the biggest benefits of owning your platform—is to begin building your email list. Social media is great for visibility, but your email list is where true connection and conversion happen. Unlike social platforms, your email list is yours to keep with no need to fight algorithms or worry about being shadow banned; meaning that your account and content can be blocked without you even realizing it. It's a direct line of communication between you and the people who've shown interest in what you offer. To get started, include a clear, visible sign-up form on your site and (ideally) pair it with a valuable freebie such as a checklist, guide, workbook, or discount code to incentivize subscriptions. It's a powerful exchange offering visitors value and insight while you simultaneously collect their contact information as a way to stay in touch, nurture relationships, and guide them toward future offerings.

In short, your website isn't just a digital business card; it's the true foundation for everything else and where people learn who you are, what you do, and why it matters. It's where they can connect with you, hire you, purchase from you, and/or join your community. It's where you create consistency and continuity outside of the (often chaotic) social media world.

So don't wait! Get started. Make it simple. Make it clean. Above all else, make it *yours*.

I know this sounds like a lot, but rest assured: you don't have to do it all at once! Feel free to start small, at least pursuing your LLC and EIN number at a minimum. Things pop up quickly in life as we all know, and in taking these steps, you give yourself somewhere to land should the unexpected occur. Maybe it's not so much about a loss though, per se. Maybe you're just like me and have reached a point where you realize you've gotten as far as your current circumstances can take you, and it's finally time to step into the life you envision for yourself. Now, you have somewhere to go.

CHAPTER 9

INTUITION

If you're longing to live a life that feels more harmonious, more grounded, and more aligned—where you're not constantly running into the same roadblocks or feeling like you're pushing uphill every single day— then do yourself a powerful favor: start trusting your intuition. Not just a hunch or fleeting feeling, it's a built-in guidance system and inner compass uniquely tuned to your truth. It exists for a reason as the part of you that picks up on subtle cues your mind may not yet understand, gently nudging you toward what feels right and away from what doesn't. It doesn't shout, but it's always speaking. The question is: are you *listening*?

The problem is, though, that many of us are taught to silence this voice having been conditioned to believe logic is king and decisions must be backed by data, spreadsheets, or a 10-point plan. We tell ourselves, *If I can't explain it or prove it, it must not be real*. This isn't

131

always true, though! In fact, some of the most successful people in the world will tell you their biggest breakthroughs came from following a gut instinct, an inner knowing perhaps not justified on paper.

We live in a world that celebrates strategy, structure, and rational thinking; while these things absolutely have their place, they aren't meant to completely override the wisdom that lives inside of you. In relying on logic alone, we often end up choosing what's safe, what's expected, and/or what looks good on paper but may not necessarily align with our spirit. Intuition often whispers before logic catches up, showing up as a sense of unease when something looks perfect on the surface but doesn't *feel* right deep down. Perhaps it's that burst of inspiration urging you to try something new even if it seems risky or unconventional. That's not foolishness—it's your internal wisdom trying to guide you toward purpose and fulfillment.

Here's the thing, though: intuition isn't about logic. It's about *feeling*, those quiet whispers inside, gut feelings, and goosebumps: physical cues that something is either in alignment or otherwise. Yet, we often push these instincts aside and dismiss them as irrational or unfounded. I learned this lesson the hard way while heading to Newark Airport recently. Not an airport I frequent much, I punched its address into my GPS at 5 a.m. as to not risk taking a wrong turn in the dark and trusting technology to get me there.

Unbeknownst to me, a car service company had apparently cleverly optimized it's listing to show up as "Newark Airport" in GPS. Not noticing the difference, I started driving—following the calm, reassuring voice of the GPS—and neared what I thought was my route to the NJ Turnpike. GPS, however, instructed me to veer off onto a side street.

Something felt wrong.

Every fiber of my being told me, *This isn't right.* Instead of trusting that instinct, though, I tried to rationalize. *Maybe there's construction up ahead,* I thought to myself. *GPS must know a better route.* Even though I knew the general direction of the airport, I allowed the GPS to override my internal compass and so spent the next 12 minutes winding through the back streets of Jersey City—growing increasingly anxious as I realized I was heading nowhere near the airport. When I finally pulled up to a nondescript building that was supposedly my "destination," I came face to face with the car service company masquerading as Newark Airport.

I felt a wave of frustration and, more than that, embarrassment. How could I have ignored all the signs? My gut had told me something was off at least five times during that detour, my body physically reacting as well with tension in my shoulders and a knot in my stomach. Yet, I pushed on. Why? Because I'd trusted external guidance over my own internal knowing. Thankfully, I had enough time to backtrack and still made my flight; but the incident stuck with me as the perfect metaphor for how we so often live our lives.

How many times have you trusted some sort of GPS in your own life rather than listen to what your gut is telling you? You're following a path—whether in your career, relationship, or with respect to a life choice—yet something just feels *off*, your gut telling you you're not heading in the right direction. Rather than pause and listen, though, you push forward: trusting your "GPS" whether that means societal expectations, the advice of well-meaning friends, or even outdated beliefs you've internalized over the years.

After all, we're conditioned from a young age to follow pre-defined "scripts": go to school, get a good job, climb the corporate ladder, get married, buy a house, have kids, retire. Deviating from said script can feel like going off the map entirely—which is terrifying—but what if the directions you're following don't lead to where you want to go in the first place?

I remember one conversation I had with a friend who was deep into her corporate career and had done everything "right." She'd climbed every rung of the corporate ladder, made the sacrifices, and put in the hours: the very definition of "success" on the surface. One day, however, she confided in me that she felt empty. "It's as if I climbed all the way to the top only to realize I'd leaned my ladder against the wrong wall," she said (a quote I in fact repurposed earlier in this very book).

That hit me hard.

It's something we in fact do quite often, pouring our energy into paths that don't align with our true desires simply because we're following someone else's version of success; and when we finally reach the top, we realize we're not where we want to be.

Trusting your intuition isn't easy and requires self-awareness, courage, and a willingness to go against the grain. Here are a few specific reasons why many of us struggle with it:

- Fear of Being Wrong: Not wanting to make mistakes, it feels risky to trust our intuition (which lacks the concrete validation logic provides), and we fear judgment—from others and ourselves—should we follow our gut and make a misstep.
- Desire for Approval: In looking to others for validation and knowing that going against the crowd can feel isolating, it takes immense strength to choose Path B if everyone else suggests Path A.
- Overthinking & Analysis Paralysis: With endless resources, advice columns, and "how-to" guides flooding our age of

information overload, we tend to overthink every decision—drowning out the quiet voice of intuition.

- Conditioning & Programming: We're taught from a young age to trust authority figures— parents, teachers, employers, etc.—which isn't inherently bad but can make us distrust our own instincts.

So, just how can you begin to trust your own internal GPS again? It starts with small steps...

Valuing Silence: Intuition thrives in stillness; if your mind is constantly racing, you won't hear your inner voice. Practices such as meditation, journaling, or even just sitting in silence for a few minutes a day can help here.

Listening to Your Body: Intuition often speaks via the body, and my very own intuitive leads are always accompanied by a physical reaction of some sort. Pay attention to how *your* body reacts in various situations.

Knowing Familiar Feelings: Think back to times when you ignored your gut. Creating awareness and connections to these same memories will help you to follow your intuition with more confidence moving forward.

Starting Small: Begin by using your intuition to make decisions that don't have large consequences if you're wrong, mitigating anxiety should the outcome be less than desirable. As you begin to trust your instinct with these smaller decisions more and more, then, you'll gradually become more comfortable with larger ones.

Let's go back to that ladder leaning against the wrong wall. Realizing you're on the wrong path can be terrifying, especially if you've invested years—or even decades—into whatever it is your doing. Remember, though; it's never too late to course correct. I've worked with clients in their 40s, 50s, and 60s who finally decide to pivot their lives away from someone else's GPS while beginning to trust their own. You know what? Many say it was the most liberating decision they've ever made! You don't need to have it all figured out to make a change, as simply taking the first step will get you going.

At the core of all this is self-trust. When you trust yourself, you stop needing external validation and become your own compass. Be sure to give yourself grace in the process and realize you're human, your humanity sometimes encouraging you to make a decision you shouldn't. Rather than beat yourself up about it, course correct instead!

I remember the first time I made a major life decision based purely on intuition while interviewing for a full-time environmental consultant job with three very similar companies—one much more desirable than the others by far and also the first company I interviewed with. Said company not only showed interest in hiring me but (more importantly) would be willing to sponsor me so I could get my green card. Completely sold, I decided to call off the other interviews: a terrifying decision because the powers that be could always change their minds, leaving my visa to expire with no job prospects and myself totally screwed. My logical mind screamed, *This doesn't make sense!* Friends and family questioned me. Deep down, though, I knew it was the right choice.

And it was! Not only that, but I'd wanted to avoid sending the universe conflicting messages. Why would I keep looking if I'd found exactly what I wanted? That decision led me down an unexpected path as part of a story you're all familiar with, and the more I trusted my intuition, the stronger that muscle became. As with building any other skill, the more you practice, the better you get.

Trusting your intuition also means embracing uncertainty. The path isn't always clear, and sometimes all you can see is the next step rather than the entire staircase. That's OK! In taking that first step, you'll allow the next one to appear and then the next. Just like walking through a fog, the path will reveal itself little by little as you move forward.

Remember: you already have the answers within you, your intuition your most powerful guide as your internal GPS always ready to point you in the right direction. Yes, you will undoubtedly take a wrong turn every now and then when you ignore that inner voice and end up at the wrong place. Yet, even those detours have value as teaching moments that strengthen your intuition for the next time. As you move forward in your journey, remember to listen, trust, and (most importantly) give yourself grace.

You are not lost. You are simply on your way. And the path? It's unfolding perfectly, one step at a time.

So go ahead—trust your internal GPS.

You know the way.

CHAPTER 10

GET IN ALIGNMENT

With about half of the book now behind us, it's time to address some of the more specific elements that may impact how your journey evolves. As you engage in your own unfolding to reveal what's inside, remember to give yourself grace and that it's not a sprint but a marathon— one calling for patience, resilience, and an open heart. I often felt as if my life was like a local bus, making every single stop while others zoomed by on the express after finding shortcuts to success. I, on the other hand, was stuck: inching forward slowly and methodically.

I'd often ask myself, *Why do I always have to take the long, slow haul? Why can't I just climb aboard the express like everyone else?* Yet as I began to reflect on my journey, I realized something profound: the local bus taught me lessons the express never could. Every stop, every delay, and every detour held a lesson, a moment of growth I would have missed had I rushed forward.

Looking back now, I see the value in the journey; the hard times, the challenges, and the moments when I felt like giving up were in fact the times I grew most. It's often during the most miserable and trying periods that we experience the most significant growth as the struggles shape us, mold us, and prepare us for what's to come.

I lacked a clear vision of what I wanted back in the early years, on this ride—evolving as an entrepreneur and business owner—but without a concrete plan. I was *doing*, not necessarily *knowing*. One of the biggest lessons I've learned, likewise, is that clarity comes through action not thought. You can sit and plan forever, creating vision boards, writing in journals, and meditating on your future, but none of that will give you the clarity that comes from actually doing. As previously mentioned, taking steps forward—no matter how small—casts away the fog that will begin to lift as soon as you start moving, the path becoming clearer with each step. Action, my friends, dispels uncertainty.

Learning to be relentlessly flexible is part and parcel of this, my lack of rigidity becoming my greatest asset after I stopped clinging to one specific outcome: opening myself up to new opportunities as well as doors I never knew existed. Being of service to others comes into play here as well, a unique kind of fulfillment to be had from helping others navigate challenges. I've personally found that when I focus on helping others, I find more clarity in my own path. Offer something people genuinely need, and you'll always find clients, supporters, and cheerleaders. Not about selling a product or service, it's about solving a problem, filling a gap, or making someone else's life a little easier or brighter; when I helped small business owners struggling with growth pains and marketing challenges, for example, I wasn't just offering a service but providing relief, solutions, and hope. That sense of purpose kept me going even when I felt lost in my own journey.

I mentioned earlier on how I decided to invest in a coach, a leap of faith both financially and emotionally but one that changed everything as my journey continued to unfold. While I'd been stuck in a cycle of self-doubt and woefully undercharging for my services—not fully understanding my worth—my coach helped me see the value I brought to the table. Setting my prices low due to a fear of rejection and assuming I'd find success if I made it easy for clients to say yes, the truth was I was devaluing my work and myself in the process. It was a hard truth: I was playing small, others flourishing while I continued to tread water. With my coach's guidance, I restructured my pricing, refined my services, and (most importantly) shifted my mindset: understanding that charging my worth wasn't selfish but indeed necessary for sustainability and growth.

While everything mentioned in this chapter thus far is of an optimistic nature, speaking to lessons learned and coming out better for it on the other side, I'd be remiss to not mention some specific challenges I've endured as well. One of the biggest? Breaking away from industry norms. A pervasive culture of struggle traditionally permeated the craft spirits industry, making it almost a badge of honor to bootstrap and barely scrape by.

I specifically remember walking into tasting events and seeing the same old uniform—plaid shirts, man buns, and work boots—speaking to the camaraderie in the struggle. Things like this also perpetuated a harmful narrative, however, tying industry success directly to suffering. In deciding to break this mold, I created a new business model that allowed me to represent multiple brands and charge a base fee plus commission. Though it was unheard of in the industry at the time, I knew it was the only way I could survive and (hopefully) thrive.

Unfortunately, I quickly realized this new model wasn't sustainable. To make enough to live on in NYC, I had to represent at least 10 brands—which meant hauling around 60+ pounds of bottles on my back, walking all over the city, and climbing subway stairs with heavy bags. It was physically exhausting and mentally draining, and my body wasn't up to the task. Eventually developing a hernia from carrying all that weight, I knew my health was deteriorating and that I couldn't keep going like this.

The true breaking point, however, came when two of my reps left: one moving out of state and the other going rogue while trying to snatch one of my clients. Suddenly, I was left with no team, no support, and a mountain of responsibilities. I was forced to confront the truth: this wasn't the life I wanted. I wanted nothing to do with this business I'd built, one tying me to a specific location, filling my days with physical labor, and leaving me feeling more trapped than free. It was the opposite of what I'd originally envisioned, and in that moment of crisis, I made a decision. I had to *let go*. Now, letting go certainly wasn't easy. It felt like admitting failure yet also, thankfully, was liberating; I realized I'd been clinging to a version of success that no longer served me.

Then along came 2020—and the pandemic—and I was forced to hit pause like so many others. It was in that stillness that I found clarity, stumbling into content creation almost by accident after making a simple TikTok about a beloved natural hair brand. It took off! That video led to my very first brand deal, opening up a brand-new path before I knew it. It was the very freedom I'd been craving—the ability to create, work from anywhere, and connect with brands and audiences on *my* terms. I also started consulting, finally leveraging my years of experience and knowledge and charging what I was worth this time around without the overhead of my previous company.

I'd done it: I was finally working in alignment with my purpose.

The biggest lesson I learned through all of this? Flexibility and giving yourself grace are key. Life rarely goes as planned, which in fact isn't a bad thing as it's those same detours that lead us exactly where we're meant to be. There's no need to have it all figured out right now. Start where you are, take the first step, and trust that clarity will come as you move forward; and remember, your journey is uniquely *yours* and shouldn't mirror anyone else's. Keep going, stay true to your vision, and give yourself grace to evolve along the way.

The value of experience is all part of this as well. Over the years, I've realized that every single lesson, no matter how painful or challenging, has added to my reservoir of knowledge: my superpower! One of the things that pains me most is hearing older individuals— especially seniors—say they no longer have anything to offer. That couldn't be further from the truth! Experience is invaluable, information currency. You simply need to connect the knowledge you've gathered over your lifetime with the people who need it, which is precisely why I started my podcast *Live, Learn, Leverage*: highlighting how we can all use our experiences to help others and create meaningful impact.

You'll also want to invest in yourself, one of the best decisions I've personally ever made. Back in 2012, I

145

bought my first online program designed specifically for solo entrepreneurs. I had zero business experience at the time—my background in architecture and environmental technology, not exactly the perfect resume for someone starting NYC food crawls—and needed guidance. That course became my lifeline and offered lifetime access so I could revisit the material as necessary, and while maybe 20% of it initially applied to me, it became more relevant as I grew and my business evolved. When I launched Tastes Brands years later, I logged back in and unearthed brand-new insights pertinent to the new *me*: in a different place with new skills and experiences. The most valuable aspect I can share with the benefit of hindsight is how information I obtained 12+ years ago feeds valuable actions I take now. Why? Because although the information remains the same, I myself am not with a lot more experience and knowledge paving the way for a totally different context than I had previously. That's the beauty of investing in yourself, which keeps paying dividends long after you make the initial investment.

Success means playing the long game with no shortcuts nor express bus—and that's okay. Every stop, detour, and unexpected twist and turn adds depth and richness to your journey. When you finally reach your destination, you'll realize it wasn't about getting there quickly but instead about who you became along the way. As you move forward, remember:

- Give yourself grace. You're doing the best you can.

- Be flexible. Your path will change, and that's okay.

- Invest in yourself. It's the best investment you'll ever make.

- Stay true to your purpose. It's your guiding light.

- Most importantly, enjoy the ride.

Not about racing to the finish line, life's about savoring every moment along the way. You've got this, so keep going, and remember: the local bus may chug along slowly, but it's filled with lessons, stories, and experiences that will shape you in ways the express never could.

This is your journey. Own it. Love it. Let it unfold.

CHAPTER 11

WHAT IS YOUR "WHY"?

Let's get right to the heart of it. What is your *why*? I want you to really sit with this question for a moment, because here's the truth: this journey you're about to embark on, whether you're launching a new business, pivoting your career, or following a passion project, it certainly won't be easy.

I'm not here to sugarcoat anything and am instead committed to always being open, authentic, and honest with you—believing in positivity but not selling fairy tales. After all, there's a difference between staying optimistic and selling someone a story that glosses over the challenges. I'll by no means assert that if you just "think positive," everything will magically work out. That's not how it goes.

Pursuing your dreams is hard work, calling for courage, resilience, and a deep-rooted sense of purpose. It means waking up one day and saying to yourself, *I'm doing this for me. I need to answer the call that's been living in my soul for far too long*. This is no small feat! Knowing your why is what will carry you through the inevitable storms that will brew and hit you along the way. Things will get tough, filled with moments when you'll question everything and feel like giving up. It's in those moments, though, that your why becomes your anchor.

I was a one-woman operation when I first entered the craft spirits world and part of a tiny team at my peak. With three people in sales and four on the tasting team, we were boutique in every sense of the word. It felt like David versus Goliath, myself pegged as David's little sister. Despite our size, however, we built a reputation based on integrity and a niche focus grounded in selling craft spirits. That was it. I took that responsibility seriously because my company was its own brand, and despite our small size, treated it as a premium offering with high standards: a principle I want *you* to adopt from day one.

You are your brand, whether you're a solo entrepreneur, coach, content creator, or operate a product-based business. When people search for your name, what do you want them to see? What kind of reputation do you want to cultivate? Every interaction, piece of content, and product reflects on *you*. That's why I was so meticulous about my team, knowing even one weak link

149

could tarnish the reputation I'd worked so hard to build. I had zero tolerance for mediocrity.

Rather than just hand new team members a manual and wish them luck, I created the most rigorous training program you could imagine featuring an entire month's worth of skill-building right in my apartment. Every. Single. Day. We went through product knowledge, sales techniques, and brand storytelling, newbies learning everything from the ABCs of vodka to the complexities of mezcal, gin, bourbon, and whiskey. Beyond just knowing how to pour a drink, they needed to be experts; simply being average doesn't cut it in such a niche market. My own reputation, meanwhile, was on the line.

Unfortunately, by the time many of my alcohol clients found me they'd already been burned—having had bad experiences with distributors who'd promised the world but delivered little. These brands had poured their hearts and souls into their products only to watch them collect dust on warehouse shelves, lost amongst a portfolio of 40,000+ SKUs.

One of the biggest disconnects in the spirits industry— as with many others—is the lack of realization that big distributors make the same promises to every brand. Whether you're Tito's or a small-batch craft distiller, they'll ramble on about getting your product into stores and bars; but what *really* happens? The big names, the ones that sell themselves, get all the attention. Why?

Because they don't require effort. A sales rep can simply walk into a store, take a reorder for Tito's, and walk out with a commission. It's easy, fast, and it pays. As for that craft vodka you poured your heart into? It sits on the shelf, unnoticed—not because it's a bad product but because no one is telling its story.

That's where I came in, filling that gap and telling those stories. I made sure the brands I worked with got the attention they deserved. Let me be completely transparent, though: this work was *exhausting*, and I realized time and again that I was driving myself into the ground.

When I first started in the craft spirits world all those years ago, my why was simple. I saw a gap and wanted to fill it, helping small brands so often overlooked. It felt good and was meaningful, but over time, that same why started to shift. The industry was sucking me dry, and by the end of 2019, I found myself questioning everything— carrying the weight of my entire team on my shoulders as clients haggled over pricing and/or didn't value the work we were doing for them.

I remember one brand in particular—one I admittedly shouldn't have taken on in the first place—who constantly nitpicked my fees, trying to score discounts and pushing for more while paying less. I let it slide, making excuses and telling myself it was all part of the hustle; but deep down, I knew better. By the end of that year, I felt completely depleted and wasn't following my why anymore. I was just trying to survive.

It's important to recognize that your why will evolve—and that's okay! What drives you today may not be what drives you five years from now. In the early days, my why was driven by obligation: to my clients, my team, and my own reputation. As for now? My why is driven by purpose. Today, I focus on empowerment and helping people like you find your path, build your brand, and navigate the complexities of entrepreneurship with confidence. It's also about impact, extending beyond income as part of a life-changing shift.

One of the most important lessons I've learned along the way is the power of authenticity. I've had my fair share of insecurities, after all, like my battle with hormonal acne well into adulthood. Imagine being a lifestyle model, showing up to set bare-faced with skin covered in hyperpigmentation. It's not fun. Here's the irony, though: those same insecurities opened doors for me. Turns out brands were specifically seeking models with hyperpigmentation to showcase their skincare products, and I ended up landing lucrative contracts—not in spite of my skin challenges but *because* of them. It's a powerful lesson: what we perceive as flaws are often the exact things that make us relatable and valuable, our authentic selves (imperfections and all) our greatest asset. People don't connect with perfection. They connect with *realness*.

So, as you reach the end of this chapter, I encourage you to pause for a moment—not to rush ahead but to instead sit with what's stirring in you right now. Take a deep breath and ask yourself, with intention and honesty: *What is my why?* Not about surface-level answers the world wants to hear, it's about *you*. What lives beneath the layers of titles, responsibilities, and expectations? What truth do you hold that no one else can name for you? What is the deeper reason that compels you to keep going, even on days when everything in you want is to quit? What gets you out of bed on the most difficult mornings? What tugs at your soul, even when it doesn't make sense on paper? What vision, hope, or cause keeps whispering to you, refusing to be silenced?

That is your why.

It may not reveal itself all at once and might show up as a quiet pull, a spark of curiosity, or a feeling that "there's something more." Sometimes it's rooted in pain you've overcome or a problem you feel called to solve. However it arrives, know that your why is your anchor in the storm and your light in the darkness. It's what will carry you when the fear creeps in and the path feels uncertain. When you fully embrace it, your why will become the heartbeat of everything you create moving forward.

So go find it. Reconnect with it. Nurture it. Let it take root in your daily choices as it guides your direction and fuels your fire. Purpose doesn't always arrive in grand gestures and instead often begins with one courageous decision to honor what matters most.

The world awaits what only *you* can bring to it. When you move based on your why, you don't just find clarity. You create alignment and meaning. You create your own table ,which is precisely where everything begins.

CHAPTER 12

CRAFT A COMPELLING STORY

Ever hear the phrase "Stories sell"? It's true! Stories are powerful connectors, bridging gaps between people and products and creating emotional links. Beyond just telling someone about a product, service, or brand, stories tie an individual to a product and—more importantly—to the reason behind the same. This is precisely why storytelling is such a crucial branding and sales element; it's a means to connect you to your audience and make your offering relatable, memorable, and (ultimately) desirable.

When I wrote *Discovering the New York Craft Spirits Boom*, I told the stories of 30 distillers sprinkled from Brooklyn to the Finger Lakes as my entry point into the alcohol industry. Before that, no one really knew me in the space beyond my work as a promotional model and brand ambassador. Writing that book was my reinvention and how I established my identity in an industry where I was essentially starting from scratch.

The process of writing allowed me to immerse myself in the world of these distillers and learn their stories: why they chose to distill, origins of their farms, their unique production methods, and the passion behind their craft. These weren't just faceless brands; they were people with dreams, struggles, and deep-rooted connections to their products. When it came time to actually sell their products in New York City—one of the most competitive markets in the world—then, I was armed with more than just a sales pitch and had *stories*. Those stories became the most powerful tool in my arsenal.

If you're familiar with Manhattan, you know how densely packed it is and how precious retail space is— especially when it comes to liquor stores. Shelf space is limited, competition fierce. Not only were most of the stores I visited teeny-tiny, but my portfolio was filled with unknown brands; and so I'd walk into these establishments and try to convince owners to clear shelf space for products with zero name recognition and (in many cases) a higher price point than household brands.

Imagine walking into a liquor store where Tito's, Grey Goose, Ketel One, and Belvedere practically sell themselves. Why would a store owner replace one of these tried-and-true bestsellers with an unknown vodka from the Hudson Valley—especially when it costs $5 to $10 more per bottle? The *story*, that's why!

In approaching these store owners and buyers, I didn't just pitch a product; I shared the story behind the product, talking about the distiller who'd left his corporate job to follow his passion and create small-batch, organic vodka. I explained how grains used in the spirit were sourced from a local family farm and how the distillery employed sustainable practices supporting the regional economy. Not stopping there, I shared my own story too—how I'd written a book about the craft-distilling boom, fallen in love with these brands and their missions, and saw an opportunity to help them grow—and made it crystal clear I wasn't just another salesperson trying to hit a quota but instead genuinely invested in supporting local businesses and bringing unique products to market.

It was an approach grounded in *connection*, bridging gaps between the distiller, myself, the buyer, and (eventually) the end customer. Think about it. When that store sells that vodka to a customer, it's not just selling a bottle of alcohol but indeed the story behind it as well. "Wanna hear something cool? This vodka is made at a small distillery in upstate New York where the owner grows his own grains and distills everything by hand," the shop owner might say. Suddenly, that $40 bottle feels special. It has a narrative. When that same customer invites friends over for a martini-infused game

157

night, guess what she'll do? Yep, share the story too! This is precisely how stories sell, transforming ordinary products into meaningful experiences.

One of the most rewarding aspects of this process was seeing how stories didn't just sell products but also bred experiences. Since many of the distilleries I worked with were local to New York State, customers often planned day trips or weekend getaways to visit the distilleries they'd discovered through these stories: feeling connected, invested, and proud to support local businesses. Noting how their purchases directly impacted these local enterprises and economies, they felt good about spending more—not just buying a product but in fact investing in a community. That connection? A powerful motivator.

If you're building a product-based business (whether food, clothing, home goods, or something else entirely), knowing your "why" is crucial for sharing the story behind what you're selling. Why did you create this product? What problem does it solve? What inspired you to bring it to life? Your "why" is what sets you apart in this respect as the factor driving people to choose your product over a less expensive, more well-known alternative.

If you're venturing into a service-based business (e.g., coaching or consulting), meanwhile, the story becomes even more personal as you yourself are the brand. You might ask yourself: *Why would anyone want to work with me? What makes me qualified?* I hear this question all the time, and I get it—imposter syndrome is real! Yet the following statement I shared earlier, has stuck with me and might resonate with you too. You are most qualified to serve the person you used to be. Think about that for a second. If you've overcome challenges, learned hard lessons, and/or navigated complex life experiences, you've gleaned valuable insights someone else is desperately searching for. Even if you're not where you ultimately want to be, you're still further along than someone else as an invaluable guide in return.

Don't underestimate your journey: every struggle, success, and stumble equipping you with the wisdom to help others. Still figuring things out? That's OK! People crave your voice, perspective, and story. Authentic sharing and storytelling is necessary to connect with them as your most powerful trust-building tool. People don't want to be sold to; they want to *connect*, feeling seen, heard, and understood. This connection only happens when you're real and vulnerable. Thinking about becoming a coach or consultant? Focus on telling your story in a way that highlights your journey, both the highs and lows. Share challenges you've faced, how you navigated them, and what you learned along the way. This creates relatability and shows others you "get it" because you've been there too.

One of the biggest challenges people face while building a brand is the desire to stay private. I completely understand that, as exposing your story to public eyes and ears can feel vulnerable and uncomfortable. Here's a hard truth, though: you can't be profitable and private at the same time. If you want to build a business that connects with people—whether you're selling a product, service, or personal brand— you must be willing to put yourself out there. People need to know who you are, what you stand for, and why they should choose *you*.

A big hurdle to entrepreneurship, likewise, is a fear of being seen—especially in the digital space. While having an online presence can feel overwhelming (particularly if you're not tech-savvy or comfortable being on camera), the good news is that building an online brand has never been easier. So many user-friendly platforms with pre-designed templates make creating a website incredibly simple these days, meaning you don't need to be a tech expert to get yourself online; you simply need to *start*.

I always tell people, "If you can color between the lines and connect the dots, you can build your own website." Most platforms also offer stellar customer support on a 24/7 basis, making help just a phone call or chat away if you happen to get stuck. I myself have reached out to reps on the other side of the world whether I'm building a site at 3 pm or 3 am, so it is indeed possible.

The key is to start *somewhere*. Get your story out there, sharing who you are, what you do, and (most importantly) why you do it. Whether you're selling a product, a service, or yourself as a brand, let me reiterate: storytelling is your most powerful tool, differentiating you in a crowded marketplace and helping people connect with you on a deeper level. Never shy away from telling your story, even the messy parts! Those are often the pieces that resonate most. The goal isn't to be perfect; it's to be authentic. Because at the end of the day, people don't buy products or services—they buy stories, connections, and emotions. *Your* story is exactly what someone out there needs to hear.

I'm such a strong proponent of self-proficiency when it comes to personal or professional development— especially as it relates to branding, marketing, and having an online presence—because we constantly grow and evolve as we craft our stories. This process should feel empowering, not limiting.

Why? Because making changes on your own gives you the freedom to act on your ideas in real time as you tweak your messaging, try out new content, and experiment with your brand's voice without waiting on someone else's timeline or worrying about another invoice. That kind of freedom is liberating and gives you space to actually grow your business.

Also keep in mind ideas don't abide by a set schedule when you're building your brand or business; inspiration can (and will!) strike at odd hours, even at two o'clock in the morning. Believe me, I've been there. In those moments while the creative energy is flowing, capture and implement said ideas—perhaps updating your website, tweaking a headline, adding a new service, or updating your bio—without balking at the fear of what it will cost you and thus stifling your creativity. When decision-making is driven by money rather than growth, guess what? You end up making less money. It's a vicious cycle that can kill momentum before it even starts.

Let me be clear: I'm not saying you should never hire a developer or designer. I've worked with some amazing ones over the years and still collaborate with them today—especially for highly specialized projects beyond my expertise. When it comes to day-to-day updates and edits, though (things like changing copy, adding a new blog post, or updating an image), I handle all of that myself. You should, too! Especially when you're just starting out.

I *also* know tech can feel overwhelming at times, especially if you're someone who doesn't naturally gravitate toward it; but the truth is it's never been easier to create and manage your own online presence, most website platforms user-friendly and built specifically for non-techies. Many offer drag-and-drop interfaces, beautiful pre-designed templates, and 24/7 customer support for when you get stuck. If you can color between the lines and connect the dots, you can absolutely build your own site.

Does the idea of content creation, marketing, and/or building your online presence still feel intimidating? Let me make it easier for you! Head to www.doltam.com to check out a number of free programs designed specifically to help people like you overcome such challenges with resources that address common content creation and marketing pain points—whether you want to craft compelling brand stories, understand social media strategy, etc. They're 100% free and there to support you as you navigate this process.

Now, I know some of you might still grimace at the thought of building a website. Maybe it feels like too big of a leap—and that's okay! Social media is there too as a great way to start building your online presence, especially in the early stages when you're still figuring things out. Platforms like Instagram, Facebook, TikTok, and YouTube offer incredible opportunities to share your story, connect with your audience, and build a following. Remember, though, that you'll need to be mindful of each platform's unique audience and culture.

For example, the way you communicate on Facebook will differ from how you engage on TikTok: the former attracting a slightly older demographic that values community and connection whereas the latter is fast-paced, video-driven, and often centered around trends and entertainment. Instagram, meanwhile, focuses heavily on visuals. As for YouTube, the video-centric platform is great for long-form content and tutorials. Tailoring your message to fit the nuances of each is essential and requires you steer clear of a one-size-fits-all approach, adapting your storytelling style per the expectations of each audience.

While social media is a great starting point, allow me to repeat a word of caution: you don't own your following on these platforms, which can change their algorithms, restrict your account, or (worse) shut down completely at any given moment. I know I have said all of this before, but it bears repeating since it's very easy to be lulled into a false sense of security depending on social platforms. Never forget those times when Facebook and Instagram went down globally for hours. Or how TikTok has faced legal scrutiny with rumors swirling about potential bans in some countries. If your entire business is built solely on a social media platform and said platform disappears or changes the rules, what happens to your brand? It disappears with it.

This is precisely why I preach about the importance of having a website—your own little corner of the Internet—is so important as a centralized hub where your audience can find you no matter what happens on social media. It also gives you full control over your content, messaging, and sales processes.

Moreover, relying exclusively on social media stifles your ability to collect and organize valuable customer information. Think about it. If people find you on Instagram in the absence of a website link, where do they go? How can they sign up for your newsletter and learn more about your services or products? It's simple; they *can't*. Do you want to risk losing these connections?

Enter the email list, another crucial brand-building element that's a direct line to your audience—no algorithms, no middlemen, just a powerful tool for building relationships, nurturing leads, and ultimately converting followers into paying customers. More specifically, an email list gives you the ability to:

1. Nurture potential clients: As people may follow you on social media but aren't always ready to buy right away, email gives you a way to stay in touch and build trust over time.

2. Share exclusive content and offers: You can use email to give subscribers special access to

resources, discounts, and/or behind-the-scenes content they can't get anywhere else.

3. Control your messaging: Unlike with social media where content might get buried in someone's feed, emails land directly in a person's inbox for top-of-mind awareness.

Even better? Building an email list need not be complicated! You can start with a simple one-page website (i.e., a landing page) that offers something of value in exchange for someone's email address—perhaps a free guide, discount code, or access to an exclusive webinar. No need to be fancy! As I always like to say, "Progress over perfection."

As for the core message I want you to take away, it's this:

You must own your brand's future.

While relying solely on social media or third-party platforms puts your business at risk, taking the time to build your own website, grow your email list, and understand how to manage your online presence allows you to take back control. Not a tech wizard? No worries! Tools available today mean you can build something functional and beautiful—that gives you the freedom to grow and evolve—without constantly worrying about costs/limitations or hiring expensive developers for every little change. Most importantly, you'll give your audience a *home*: a place where they can find you, connect with you, and (ultimately) buy from you.

I know this process can feel overwhelming, especially when you're just starting out, but remember... It's not about being perfect. It's about making *progress*. Start small. Build that one-pager website. Create your first email list. Post consistently on one or two social media platforms. As you gain confidence and momentum, you can expand on and refine your strategy.

The most important thing? Just *start*. Every moment you wait is a missed opportunity to share your story, connect with your audience, and grow your brand; and if you need any support along the way, remember that I'm here for you! Whether with respect to the free resources on my website or the insights shared in this book, my goal is to help you take those first steps with confidence.

So go ahead and do it. Your future self will thank you.

CHAPTER 13

PERFECTION IS WHERE DREAMS GO TO DIE

It's one of my favorite sayings and something I believe with all my heart: "Perfection is the place where dreams go to die." Why? Because perfection doesn't exist. It's a mirage, something we keep chasing but can never actually catch. Waiting for the stars to align before you start that project, launch that business, or make that life change? Prepare to wait a very, very long time.

The goal, instead, is progress over perfection. Just get it *done*. Write the book, start the business, create the art—whatever it is, do it now and forget about flawlessness. Done is always better than perfect, which will quite frankly never arrive.

When I think about the many phases of my career and the different things I've done, one constant has driven me: the desire to feel connected to my work, which in turn creates an environment of learning that paves the way for passion and purpose. When you're engaged and growing, your desire and attitude will push you past the challenges as you gain experience that becomes invaluable over time.

One problem with chasing perfection is that it often leads to paralysis. You end up stuck, overthinking every little detail and getting nothing done in the process. While it may sound harsh, it's simply the truth. Those always waiting for the "perfect" moment or "perfect" product risk never starting at all.

Now, let me be clear: I'm not endorsing sloppiness or carelessness and fully believe in doing things the right way. One of my core values, likewise, is that how you do one thing is how you do *everything*. Always do your best yet also recognize when the pursuit of perfection is holding you back. We're all perfectly imperfect, which is precisely what makes us unique—our flaws and quirks part of who we are. A funny story from last summer illustrates this perfectly...

I'd just finished shooting content in my apartment and decided to take my dog for a walk. I was wearing a simple pair of shorts and enjoying the weather when I saw a woman walking toward us with two dogs. Our pups stopped to sniff each other, as they do, and we struck up a conversation.

The woman exclaimed, "My God, you're flawless! Your skin is so beautiful!"

Caught off guard, I blurted out, "What? Me? Really? Well, it's actually just IT Cosmetics."

She laughed and asked, "Do you put it all over your body too?"

"No," I replied, a little embarrassed.

She wasn't having it. "But look at your arms and your legs—your skin is glowing!"

What did I do? I deflected again. "I really appreciate you saying that, but I actually have issues with hyperpigmentation."

She wrinkled her nose, looked me dead in the eye, and said, "What is wrong with you?"

I burst out laughing. It was such a pure, honest moment that made me realize how quick we are to downplay compliments. Why couldn't I just accept her kind words? Why did I feel the need to point out my flaws rather than reply with a simple "Thank you"? It's simple: the same inner voice that drives us to seek perfection also feeds our insecurities. Opposite sides of the same coin, the voice that says "You need to be perfect" is the same one whispering "You're not good enough."

I'm sharing this because I'm on this journey with you. We're *all* learning. Even in that moment and as someone who preaches self-love and acceptance, I failed to fully receive a compliment and accept the positive energy the universe was offering me—and I had to laugh at myself! There I was, always talking about embracing positivity and the gifts life gives us and yet when presented with a beautiful, genuine compliment, all I could focus on were my perceived flaws.

This experience brings to mind another pivotal moment in my life, when I decided to buy my first house. It was February 2003, right around the time Auntie Lucille had given me *The Game of Life and How to Play It*: a book that shifted my mindset and helped me realize how powerful our words and thoughts truly are. I was living in a Long Island apartment at the time and working crazy long hours. My landlady, a lovely person, often told me how much she appreciated having me as a tenant. "You're the best tenant I've ever had. I hope you never leave," she'd say.

One day, as we were chatting, I asked if I could get a dog. I'd always loved animals, especially dogs, and really wanted one. Smiling, she replied with a disappointing yet understandable answer. "I know you'd take great care of a dog, but I unfortunately can't allow pets. You work long hours, and it's just not something I can approve."

I didn't argue and instead shrugged and said (half-jokingly), "Well, I guess I just need to buy my own house then." They were just words at the time, but there was indeed emotion behind them: my want for a dog fueling my statement.

Two weeks later, my offhand comment turned into something much bigger. I'd just started a new job and thought to myself, *Why not, though? Everyone else owns a house. How hard can it be?* Funny enough and out of the blue, my landlady had decided to sell her own house and asked if I was interested. I was floored. She believed in me, even before I fully believed in myself, and deemed me capable of becoming a homeowner. That belief gave me the confidence to kickstart my house search in earnest.

In the end, I didn't buy her house. It just wasn't the right fit, but that moment set the wheels in motion all thanks to an emotion-filled statement I'd made without realizing its power. The lesson? Our words carry *energy*. Things we say, even casually, can shape our reality— which is why it's so important to speak with intention and surround ourselves with people who believe in us, even when we're still figuring things out. Sometimes, it takes someone else's belief to spark our own.

So, how exactly does this all tie back to perfection? It's simple: waiting for perfection holds us back. Whether we're accepting a compliment, starting a business, or pursuing a dream, the need for everything to be "just right" keeps us from moving forward. When we embrace progress over perfection and start before we feel fully ready, however, that's when the magic happens. We grow, we learn, and we realize the imperfections are what make the journey meaningful.

So, the next time you catch yourself awaiting the perfect moment or doubting your worth, remember this: You are already enough. Right now. As you are. If someone offers you a compliment? Just say thank you.

Back then I felt as if I was just trying to figure life out, with no real roadmap nor sense of how to do anything "the right way." I was simply moving forward, plodding along if I'm being honest, with no inkling of perfection nor crystal-clear clarity in anything I was doing. I took action anyway, moving forward and focusing on progress over perfection. Small steps and tiny wins here and there, that was my approach.

When I'd share my plans with people around me, their reactions were filled with disbelief. "How can you afford that? You're so young, and you don't have anyone supporting you. How could you possibly pull this off?" The truth? I had no idea, no master plan, no step-by-step guide. All I knew was that I was going to figure it out.

One of my greatest blessings during that time was that I wasn't weighed down by a need to have all the answers and didn't overthink every little detail. I simply moved forward, trusting that things would come together as they should. A lot of people tried to talk me out of my plans, telling me they didn't make sense, and in hindsight they weren't completely wrong.

Owning a house all by myself on Long Island while making $40,000 a year was definitely not the most financially sound decision. I worked a ridiculous number of hours just to keep up with the mortgage, and my house became more of a place to sleep than a place to live. I was out all the time, working multiple jobs just to afford it and eat something other than Cheerios. I'm glad I took that leap, though, because here's the thing: we can manifest incredible things when we remove the limits from our minds and vision. Stop waiting for the "perfect" moment (which will never come), and take the first step—even if it's small, even if it's messy—to create momentum as a signal to the universe saying, "I'm serious about this. I'm ready. I'm committed." Trust me: the universe will respond. People, opportunities, and information will start showing up, often in unexpected ways, to help you take the next step and then the one after that and so on.

A related and equally important lesson? Be mindful of who you share your dreams with. Not everyone will understand your vision, and please—whatever you do— as I've also mentioned before, don't ask for directions from someone who's never been where you want to go. It is one of the fastest ways to get lost. People might mean well, but if they haven't walked the path you're on, their advice may come from a place of fear or limitation rather than possibility.

Their doubts need not become your doubts; just because something didn't work out for someone else doesn't mean you will experience the same. You are on your own unique journey. Value yourself, trust yourself, and know that every experience—whether a success or a stumble—is a stepping stone. Stay relentlessly flexible. Plans will change and life will throw curveballs, and that's okay.

Many folks have a difficult time with this concept, and I've seen such rigidity play out time and again, especially in business. Some people create detailed plans and then cling to them, even when it's clear they're no longer working—so attached to their original vision and blinded to brand-new opportunities right in front of them. I remember telling one client: "Life is presenting you with a better option. Can't you see it?" Stuck on the original blueprint, though, and needing time to "think about it," he learned the opportunity had unfortunately passed him by after finally coming around.

I've had my own personal experience with this, most notably when a vacation in Italy taught me a powerful lesson in flexibility.

A group of us had planned an incredible boat trip along the Italian coast, inspired by a similar trip we'd taken the previous year. It was supposed to be perfect—sun, sea, and pure relaxation. Landing in Rome, though, we were hit with unexpected news: the boat was still in the shipyard in need of repair, and no one had bothered to tell us. So, there we were, all five/six of us in the Italian Riviera in the middle of summer with no place to stay. The shock was real, our perfectly planned vacation falling apart before our very eyes.

This is precisely where flexibility came in. Pivoting our plans and arriving to the rental car counter, we learned all the vehicles on the lot were manual transmission. A hindrance for many Americans, this challenge was no match for yours truly who'd learned to drive with a stick shift back in Grenada; the time had come to put that knowledge and experience into action on a boat-trip-turned-road-trip adventure. It wasn't the coastal trip we'd originally planned, but it was still Italy. Why not make the most of it?

Renting a minivan, we set off on roads hugging the Italian and French Riviera coastline and went on to enjoy the trip of a lifetime following initial disaster: exploring charming towns and ancient villages, stumbling upon an incredible vineyard, and even watching a local soccer match at a cozy restaurant. Making the most of those first five days, we discovered places and took part in experiences we never would have had our original plans materialized.

It was funny, though; despite how much fun we were having, the conversation kept circling back to that lost opportunity. "Can you believe we're not on the boat? This wasn't the plan!" we'd say between sips of wine at a beautiful hillside vineyard, as if part of us couldn't fully embrace the moment—so fixated on what *should* have been.

The company wound up booking us on another boat for the last five days of the trip so we could enjoy the coastal experience we'd originally planned. It was beautiful, no doubt, but when we arrived back home and reflected on the trip, turns out our fondest memories were of our time on the road—the unexpected detour the highlight.

It was a crucial life lesson; when you're too focused on what's "supposed" to happen, you miss the beauty of what's *actually* happening. In almost letting our disappointment to not be at sea ruin what turned out to be an amazing experience on land, we were reminded that flexibility is everything. As life rarely goes according to plan, the key is to stay present and open to new possibilities while knowing detours can lead to the most beautiful destinations.

Wherever you are right now and whatever you're going through, know this: you are exactly where you're supposed to be, even if that looks nothing like what you originally envisioned. Trust the process, stay open, and most importantly, be *present*. Don't miss the magic of the moment simply because you're too focused on what "should have been."

Every experience, planned or unplanned, is an opportunity for growth. Take the first step, stay flexible, and trust that life will unfold exactly as it should.

CHAPTER 14

FIGURE OUT YOUR FINANCES

The time has come to dive into a not-so-glamorous topic: finances.

Full disclosure that I am by no means a financial advisor, consultant, or business strategist; but I'd be doing you a disservice if I didn't touch on this topic as understanding and managing finances is critical to building anything sustainable. No matter how brilliant your ideas are or how passionate you feel, none of it will come to life if your financial wherewithal falls short.

Now, I'm not sure where you are in your life right now or what brought you to this point, but I can imagine a few likely scenarios. Maybe you're frustrated with your job and feeling stuck, knowing deep down you want to pivot but don't know how to make the leap; or perhaps you're approaching retirement (or already retired) and want to leverage your years of experience to create something

179

meaningful in lockstep with your passions. Either which way, you're here because you want to bring your gifts to the world. I want to help you do that in the smartest, most mindful way possible.

When I launched my first business, I didn't just jump ship and bid adieu to my job right away. If you've followed my story, you'll remember I've always juggled multiple jobs and income streams. Even while working as an environmental consultant, I had side gigs—one of which was hosting tastings. Why? Because my salary wasn't enough to cover my mortgage, bills, and, quite frankly, a diet beyond cereal.

As for my first business, I continued working my 9-to-5 while building my side hustle for a period of two years— and let me tell you, this overlap was critical. It gave me the financial stability to make mistakes without the pressure of potentially unpaid bills, breathing room that allowed me to take risks and grow my business organically.

Not every business takes off overnight. Some ideas flourish quickly, while others require a longer gestation period. When I launched my first company in 2012, I was so excited to work in a space I loved: food and wine. It was a passion project that brought me immense joy, but transforming said passion into a sustainable business was an entirely different challenge. I made plenty of mistakes along the way but didn't have to abandon my dream when things got tough thanks to the safety net of my day job.

One of the biggest lessons I've learned, likewise, is that financial pressure can stifle creativity. When you're worried about paying rent, affording groceries, and/or covering bills, it's nearly impossible to create with a clear, focused mind—which is precisely why I always encourage people to maintain an additional revenue stream while building their business, especially in the earliest stages. Those who work remotely might already have some built-in flexibility, which is a huge advantage, but I recommend maintaining a supplemental income source until your business reaches a point where it can fully support you nonetheless.

One of the best pieces of financial advice I can give you is that if you need extra cash while building your dream, choose a side gig that doesn't drain your mental energy: ideally finding something where you can show up, do the work, get paid, and leave, all without demanding too much headspace. The last thing you want is a side hustle that starts consuming all your time and creativity—something I learned the hard way.

As mentioned earlier on in the book, I decided to operate a hair salon of sorts out of my dorm room back in college. It was the 90s, and box braids and extensions were all the rage. My offering? A cheaper, more convenient alternative to professional salons. My classmates loved it. With our campus in Suffolk County, it saved them a long trip to Brooklyn as a huge bonus.

The experience started off great. I was making good money, my weekends were booked, and I had a steady flow of clients. Soon enough, though, the business spiraled out of control. Between the flyers I'd put up and good old-fashioned word of mouth, my dorm suddenly transformed into a revolving door of clients with people knocking on my door at all hours of the day and night. Each appointment, meanwhile, consumed anywhere from two to six hours. Before I knew it, I was spending more time braiding hair than studying architecture—the reason I was there in the first place!

Residential Life eventually caught up with me and shut the whole thing down; who knew running a business out of a dorm room was against the rules? An international student, I also had no clue about taxes or the legal side of things. It was a mess, but it taught me a valuable lesson: your side gigs can easily take over if you're not careful, especially if you need the money and it's seemingly "easy" to come by. Everything comes at a cost.

It's for this very reason I suggest taking on supplemental work that doesn't involve creating something from scratch or building a client base, as to not risk losing sight of your main goal.

Your stage in life also matters. I didn't have children when I was first starting out, for example, which gave me more flexibility to take risks. Not everyone has that option, though. *Your* approach will differ if you have kids, a mortgage, or other significant responsibilities—and that's okay! It doesn't mean you can't go after your dreams; it just means you'll need a solid financial plan to do so.

Self-education—which I'm a huge believer in—comes into play here as well. When I decided to dive into entrepreneurship, I knew my vision for my life was bigger than my current circumstances. I *also* knew I needed to increase my financial literacy to make it happen. You can't run a successful business without understanding finances to some degree; beyond just selling a great product or service, you need to wrap your head around cash flow, taxes, investments, and how to plan for the future—including retirement, especially if you're starting this journey later in life. It's crucial to consider impacts to your long-term financial goals and ask yourself relevant questions such as *How will using my savings affect my retirement?* and *Do I have enough set aside to weather the ups and downs of entrepreneurship?*

I strongly encourage you to consult a financial advisor before making any major moves, combining his or her expertise with your own research; countless books and resources on financial literacy can help you get started!

183

Think you can just "hope for the best"? Think again—winging it is by no means sound financial strategy.

As for one of the most common mistakes I've seen with respect to the financial side of things, that's when people believe the story they want to hear rather than face the truth: something I experienced firsthand while working with brands desperate to break into the market. Those I'd onboard would inevitably ask, "Heather, how long will it take to start making money?" My response? Always the same: "Do you want the truth, or do you want me to tell you a nice story?"

On so many occasions, the reason they came to me in the first place was because someone else had already told them a story of some kind—one feeding their dreams and egos with zero grounding in reality. Having been promised quick success, high demand, and booming sales, they packed shipping containers full of products, sent them off to New York, and expected them to sell like hotcakes; but then nothing happened. Inventory sat untouched, money was tied up, and the "experts" who'd sold them such dreams were nowhere to be found.

By the time they reached me, then, they were under immense financial pressure and desperate for results. I made it a priority to always be honest with them though, knowing success wouldn't happen overnight. Breaking into such a market takes time, money, and patience:

requiring countless tastings, marketing efforts, and customer education before a brand can develop a loyal following and (subsequently) consistent sales.

The God's honest truth, however harsh, is that many of these brands went under simply because they'd failed to account for the gestation period—the time it takes for a product to move from the shelves into customer hands on a consistent basis—as well as the expense of holding tastings and running promotions. The time necessary for stores to reorder based on customer demand was another factor they'd missed. All of this came back to one thing: financial pressure.

The ultimate goal here is to give yourself the financial breathing room to create with freedom, not fear, so you can make decisions based on what's best for your business—with no need to panic about paying rent, for example. Whether that means maintaining a side gig, consulting a financial advisor, or spending a bit more time to plan before diving in, take the necessary steps now to succeed later and in the long term. Remember: it's not a sprint but a marathon, and the more intentional and prepared you are, the more likely you'll build something truly sustainable that aligns with your passion and supports your life.

Remember the story I shared about the client I'd considered onboarding in January 2018? The one who ignored all of my advice? Here's a bit more about that...

I always cultivated all of my relationships—with clients on the retail side, liquor stores, bars, and restaurants—with care and integrity. These folks trusted me, knowing any product I brought into their establishments was something I stood behind 100%. That trust wasn't built overnight; it came from years spent consistently showing up, ensuring products moved off the shelves, and doing whatever it took to ensure product success. I'd even do tastings myself, especially for large orders, in many cases. If a client specifically requested me by name, I was there. No excuses. That level of commitment solidified trust and made it clear I was in it for the long haul—not just to make a quick sale.

Enter that prospective client, the one who wanted me to compromise my integrity for the sake of his poorly planned decisions. In asking me to sell his product to these trusted accounts, he planned to triple the price after selling them the initial inventory. Why? Because he'd made a costly mistake previously, importing two crates of spirits through a wine importer who (by law) couldn't sell spirits without a specific license to do so. It was a detail he'd been completely unaware of, and he found himself stuck. To fix the error, he'd need to resell the crates to a licensed spirits importer and incur additional costs he intended to pass on to retailers and (ultimately) the customers themselves.

That was my breaking point, and I walked away furious as mentioned earlier. Not only had he created a mess for himself due to his own poor planning, but he expected me to clean it up while risking my own reputation in the process. Why should I compromise my integrity and the trust I'd built with my clients simply because someone else hadn't done his due diligence? It was a hard but necessary decision.

These kinds of conversations were never easy, and most potential clients didn't like hearing hard truths. They wanted quick wins and instant success, but I refused to sugarcoat reality. If someone sought faster results, I'd dial up an honest response upfront: "These are my terms. If you're not comfortable with them, that's fine. Feel free to walk away right now—no hard feelings."

What I *wasn't* willing to do, under any circumstances, was sell them a fairytale just to make them feel better— especially when they were under intense financial pressure. Some of these people had remortgaged their homes and burned through their savings to bank everything on their product's success. While I empathized with that kind of pressure, I also knew desperation breeds bad decisions.

This is precisely why I always limited my contracts to one year, knowing most brands simply didn't have the resilience or financial stability to renew over an extended period of time beyond that. When you start off on the wrong foot, especially in a product-based business, every stage of the process is impacted. Not unique to the spirits industry, it's true in any field where products are created for public consumption.

The bottom line is this: financial pressure fuels poor decisions, and desperation clouds judgment. It leads to shortcuts, bad deals, and compromises that can hurt you in the long run. Before diving into any venture, whether you're launching a product, starting a business, or even pivoting into a new career, take a moment to think it through. While you can't plan for everything (and surprises will undoubtedly come out of left field from time to time), the more thought and strategy you put in on the front end means the better positioned you'll be to handle those curveballs on the back end.

Most importantly, don't let financial pressure force you into decisions that compromise your integrity, your relationships, or your long-term vision. It's not worth it. Trust me.

CHAPTER 15

MAKE ROOM FOR THE SHIFT

Changing beliefs involves feelings of discomfort. The fact is, so many emotions begin to crop up as we fight against what we believe to be true while learning new information that goes against long-held beliefs—a natural, not uncommon reaction. I bring this up because as this plays out in our subconscious mind and we don't realize exactly what it is, it can unknowingly impede progress. Bringing it to the front of your mind, on the other hand, allows you recognize and address it head on and move forward more quickly.

When I made the decision to become a lifestyle model, for example, one particular narrative kept coming up yet I didn't realize it at the time. All of my experience up until that point required me to work really long, hard days and dedicate time, labor, and energy to get the job done right. In booking modeling jobs, though, I suddenly found myself receiving the same exact compensation for a few hours of work as I had for an entire month's worth. A disconnect formed in my mind; I was the same individual with the same work ethic receiving compensation not proportional to what I deemed the time necessary to justify it. The *effort* was very different. It's exactly how we begin to sabotage our own success.

Admittedly and as much as I hate to say this, I began to feel somewhat uncomfortable. It feels absurd to even write these words, but those were indeed the underlying emotions; I struggled to own my work because it went against everything I'd previously known to be true, leading me to believe there was something wrong with it. *I'm not working hard enough. I'm not doing enough. This is so easy. Too easy.* I began to equate this sense of effortlessness to a lack of worthiness, believing I'd be more deserving if I only worked harder.

Looking back, I can see the irrationality in what I was doing to myself—not making sense of the fact that I was making the same money simply being me and doing the job asked of me. I was paid the pre-allocated rate, absolutely no one doing me any favors, yet it somehow made me feel like *less* (if that makes any sense at all). Then there were those who'd been doing the same thing all their lives and were making 10 to 20 times more than I was; they had zero qualms! It was what they were used to. I remember one shoot when a model told me he'd never accept a job that paid less than $1k or was scheduled later than early afternoon. Those were his terms, and he had every right to own them.

Let me ask you: What are your beliefs around money? What do you deem a "reasonable" amount to be paid over a specific period of time? The lessons we're taught from an early age directly impact who we are and how we identify, impacting how we show up in the world in numerous ways; labels others have given us, values we've adopted, and our own individual beliefs all come together to create who we are, often in an unsuspecting way. You have a dream in your heart—something you genuinely want to do—and then someone comes along (likely a family member) and says, "I think you should pursue [insert different vision] instead." Before you know it, you're living a disingenuous life you don't recognize simply because you haven't given yourself permission to even contemplate a greater opportunity grounded in a skill you have or knowledge you can share. There is indeed value beyond what you can see.

Back when I was a consultant and review time came around, I was always told I had a great work ethic and always put my best food forward—without dispute. While my manager lauded my performance during one such review, in the same breath he pointed out how I'd always leave work at five o'clock since my other job started at six (a well-known fact) and then began speaking about one of my colleagues. Let's call him "Johnny." Johnny, around my age, joined the company a year and a half after me and was apparently an example of what I should strive for. My manager was very impressed with him as he'd stay until seven, eight, or sometimes even nine o'clock at night and walk out the door with him.

So you acknowledge I'm doing everything I'm supposed to do and performing well yet want me to stay two, three, or four hours after 5 pm because why exactly? Because of how this guy shows his commitment to the firm by staying late? I was perplexed, not to mention the fact that my second job prevented me from even doing that in the first place.

Johnny, meanwhile, would quite literally walk around the office chatting on his cell phone all day—with absolutely no one on the line. Not a single soul. Yep, it was all a façade. He made sure to do this "lap" every 30 to 45 minutes to make himself known and visible to the office manager before returning to his cube and playing video games. He also wouldn't get into the office until around 9:30 am or 10 am each day, something the office manager was unaware of because he entered through the equipment room near his desk.

This foolishness recently came to mind when I saw on social media he'd celebrated a significant milestone at the company. *Maybe he actually began to do real work, having survived there all these decades,* I thought to myself. The point of the story is twofold; my manager was so impressed by the ridiculous facade and fabricated image of greatness presented to him (in contrast to my tried-and-true efficiency) and, even more concerning, had asked me to live up to an expectation I knew wasn't even possible.

It's just like how we're often unaware of the narratives we believe in our own lives that simply aren't true, accepting said narration due to what the narrator says— whether society, family, friends, or even our own inner critic. Not always intentional, it's often deception by default wherein we assign value to these narratives as observers and give them power even when they don't serve us. Think about times in your life when you've tried to fit into someone else's mold, doing things just to meet others' expectations. You run a race not meant for you, ticking off boxes on a checklist someone else wrote. In those moments, you're simply existing—not living—and it's soul-crushing to the core. There's nothing more draining than doing something just for the sake of it in order to check a box. I've never been that person. If I commit to something, it's because it feels *right*, and I'll do it wholeheartedly and with integrity or not at all. While this approach isn't everyone's cup of tea, it allows me to live authentically.

Now, let's talk about making room for the shift—in mindset, energy, and purpose. This requires we confront emotions that might feel uncomfortable, especially when we begin to believe there's more out there for us:

more that we're capable of achieving. Anxiety is one of the first emotions to surface during this process, especially if you've spent most of your life as the provider, the caretaker, the person who puts everyone else first. Now, I'm not saying you need to stop providing or caring for others, just that you must realize (perhaps for the first time) if your needs are taking a back seat on a consistent basis. Not about putting yourself first or even second, you may have in fact never even placed— on the sidelines and cheering others on as they accomplish their goals while you put your own dreams on hold. While there's fulfillment and joy in supporting others, this can also lead to quiet anger and deep-seated resentment over time. You look back one day and realize that 10, 20, maybe even 30 years have passed, and you've spent all that time helping others reach their potential while ignoring your own.

Fear might also creep in as you feel the pull to step into your own light. *Can I really do this? Is it too late? Do I even know how?* Sit with those feelings. I know it's scary, but growth always starts in that space: the uncomfortable middle ground between where you are and where you want to be. There's also the challenge of the people around you. When you share your desire to pursue something new—something that breaks away from your traditional self—enthusiasm doesn't always follow, your evolution instead making others uncomfortable as it disrupts the dynamic they're used to. This can manifest as skepticism, dismissiveness, or even outright criticism.

My advice? Sit with it. Sit with your feelings, their reactions, and the tension that may arise. Don't rush to fix it or smooth things over. Be still and listen to your life's calling. You don't need to have all the answers right now, but you *do* need to set the intention—which is everything. This is where the power of language comes into play, especially when you say "I am." These two little words are among the most powerful you can speak as the subconscious mind doesn't differentiate between truth, dreams, jokes, or lies. When you say something like "I am successful" or otherwise "I am unworthy," your subconscious mind accepts these statements as fact and begins to shape your reality around these same declarations—whether they serve you or not.

That's why it's so important to be mindful of how you speak about yourself and your life. Careless words have power, and people unintentionally speak themselves into lives they don't want simply because they're not guarding their thoughts or words. Thoughts become things, and we become what we think about. When you start guarding your inner dialogue and speaking the desires of your soul, clarity will come.

Don't stress; you don't need to have it all figured out right now! What matters is that you're committed to your own unfolding. You may not even know what the questions are yet, yet you feel the answers stirring within you—which is enough to begin. I remember feeling this way for a long time, with a vision of my life and a desire to live without being tied to one place: to have the freedom to create something meaningful with my skills, talents, and ideas. I had no clue how to transform these into a viable life, though, and just knew I wanted to make a difference. It was as if I had all the answers without knowing the corresponding questions.

I eventually learned, however, that if you commit to being aggressively flexible and staying open to possibilities while moving forward with intention, the path will begin to reveal itself in time. There's no need to know exactly where you'll end up, just that your compass is pointing in the right direction. So long as you're moving toward the essence of what you want, the details will fall into place eventually.

I love the saying, "The clutches of limited perception have no power here." It's a reminder that most of our fears, doubts, and insecurities are rooted in distorted perceptions: things that aren't real. We build walls around ourselves based on assumptions and limiting beliefs, only to realize—once we confront them—that they're paper-thin. Something powerful happens when you face your fears, which will in turn fall away to reveal a stronger, more grounded, and more confident YOU. Overcoming limiting beliefs likewise creates space for your authentic self to emerge, which is when the real transformation begins.

Give yourself grace through it all. Just as you didn't get here overnight, you won't unravel years of patterns and conditioning in a single moment. It's a journey, and as with any meaningful journey, it takes time. As you transition from one mindset to another, extend that same grace to the people around you as well—who are witnessing a version of you they may not recognize. Change can be unsettling, not just for you but for them too, and there's no need to share everything all at once. Be selective, share when you feel strong and stable, and understand that not everyone will understand. That's okay!

This process sometimes reveals rifts in relationships, and you might feel as if you no longer fit in with certain friends or communities. It's a heartbreaking realization and important to remember that success shouldn't come at the cost of loneliness. True success, on the other hand, features connection, love, and belonging. Remember that not everyone is meant to walk every part of your journey with you, and some people may not understand the changes you're making. Respect their path while staying true to your own, knowing it's all okay.

Share your journey in bite-sized pieces, and let relationships evolve naturally. There's no need to

197

convince or convert people in your life, nor criticize those not growing at the same pace. We're all on our own unique journey, moving through life's twists and turns at different speeds, and you create room for deeper, more authentic connections while giving yourself and others space to grow in the absence of judgement or expectations. It's all about becoming who you were always meant to be—not who *others* expect you to be—as part of a process requiring courage, mindfulness, and (most importantly) love for yourself and those around you.

I personally know this quite well, having once lost a 14-year friendship in a way I never expected. I've actually never shared this story publicly before, but I think now is the time as it speaks to the fragility of relationships and the importance of mindfulness in how we communicate—especially during pivotal moments in our lives.

Many years ago, a close friend of mine was getting married after meeting her fiancé only six months prior and experiencing a whirlwind romance. I had been in a relationship for just over a year at the time, one that was loving and happy but lacked any long-term plans for the future. During one of our conversations, she bluntly asked me: "What's wrong with you, and what's wrong with him? You've been together all this time but still aren't engaged?"

Her words stung. Beyond just the questions themselves, the underlying judgment and insinuation there was something inherently flawed about me and my relationship simply because we weren't mirroring her timeline felt dismissive and invalidating—especially coming from someone I'd loved like a sister for over a decade.

I didn't know how to respond and was left speechless, unsure of whether I should defend myself or just let it slide. Silence won, but that moment planted a seed of hurt and distance between us. It took me almost a year to find the courage, and the right words, to tell her how much the comment hurt me. So much had changed by then, though, her marriage having ended after just eight or nine months: a painful, emotional time for her, and I didn't want to add to her burden despite my own feelings. I thus kept my hurt to myself, and the space between us only grew wider. Our friendship fractured in ways neither of us could fully mend and eventually broke altogether.

Losing that relationship taught me so much about communication, timing, and the importance of being mindful with our words, especially when we're on the receiving end of life's victories. As you evolve and celebrate your successes, heed this gentle (and important) reminder: be mindful of how you celebrate, recognizing the delicate balance between owning your success and unintentionally belittling someone else's journey. Now, I'm not suggesting you dim your light for the sake of others' comfort—playing small to accommodate such insecurities—but that your achievements are fully deserving of unapologetic celebration with mindfulness as the key. It's about celebrating with grace and sensitivity; though you're experiencing a high point, others are perhaps navigating a struggle of some kind. Not about shrinking yourself, it's about expanding your awareness and being intentional in your words and actions to ensure your celebration doesn't come at the expense of someone else's dignity or self-worth.

Many people carry invisible burdens we may never fully understand in a world chock-full of challenges, giving us an opportunity to be the light we hope to see whenever we experience joy, success, and abundance: using such moments of victory not only to uplift ourselves but also inspire and encourage others. Imagine what the world would look like if more of us approached life this way, tending to our own small plots with love, kindness, and mindfulness and then sharing that bounty with those around us. The ripple effect would be profound! In managing our own space emotionally, mentally, and spiritually, we create a sanctuary not just for ourselves but for others who may need a little extra light in their lives.

Here's the best part about it: When you live this way, you begin to see beauty beyond the surface as it radiates from your soul. A deep, abiding sense of connection, empathy, and love that can't be faked or forced, it's the kind of beauty that leaves a lasting imprint long after the initial celebration dies down.

As you step into your success, I encourage you to celebrate boldly but also compassionately. Feel proud of what you achieve but stay grounded. Be the light, remembering that sometimes the brightest lights are also the warmest and invite others in rather than push them away.

It all starts with *us*, change initiated within. In managing our own energy, intentions, and actions with care, we can create a ripple effect that extends far beyond what we ever imagined and thus contribute to a more compassionate and connected world—one mindful celebration at a time.

CHAPTER 16

DIRECTION IS MORE IMPORTANT THAN SPEED

If you read my book *Pivot: Because Life Doesn't Always Go As Planned*, you may recall me talking about meeting the person who quite literally changed my life. Dr. Lucille Farrel Scott, whom I lovingly call Auntie Lucille, was so much more than just a mentor to me; she was a guiding light during one of the darkest periods of my life.

Auntie Lucille handed me a book that would become a turning point. *The Game of Life and How to Play It* by Florence Scovel Shinn (published in 1925) became my blueprint for understanding how my thoughts, words, and actions align to shape my life: opening my eyes to how even a small lapse in intention whether in thought, speech, or deed can steer you off course and dramatically impact your life's trajectory.

To be absolutely clear, I'm not receiving compensation in return for mentioning this book or any of the others referenced in this chapter. There's no sponsorship, no hidden agenda. I'm simply sharing these insights from a place of honesty and authenticity as they were pivotal in my own journey, believing they might indeed offer something meaningful to you as well.

I'll never forget the day I received this book during what was supposed to be a time of celebration. Though I'd just landed a job as an environmental consultant, it felt as if my world was unraveling; I'd achieved something great on the surface but felt lost and disconnected on the inside. I remember sitting with Auntie Lucille, the first person to teach me the true power of words, and feeling completely overwhelmed. "Life and death are in the power of the tongue" felt like just another phrase at first, something I'd heard countless times but never truly understood, until she broke it down for me in a way that stuck.

Auntie Lucille explained how the subconscious mind doesn't understand jokes or sarcasm and takes everything you say as truth (as previously mentioned) without questioning whether you "meant it" or were "just kidding." No buffer. No safety net. When you speak carelessly and say something like "I'm so unlucky" or "Nothing ever works out for me," your subconscious listens and begins to shape your reality to match such declarations. Now, I'm not suggesting life is devoid of true pain or legitimate challenges—we need not look far to witness the world's atrocities or everyday struggles—but instead that I learned how even in our darkest moments, we have the internal power to shift our reality. Such power begins in our minds and hearts per the intentions we set.

When Auntie Lucille gave me that book, I was at my lowest point and can remember saying *God, please help me. Anything!* Not trying to make a grand spiritual statement, I was simply broken and needed help and share this now not to push my beliefs but rather honestly divulge where I was at that time. Something remarkable happened then though, something I didn't fully understand until years later. Slowly but surely, things in my life began to shift. Have you ever reached a point where you feel stripped down to nothing, emotionally, mentally, and/or spiritually? As if your heart and soul are laid bare with nowhere left to hide? That's exactly where I was. In that place of complete surrender, something powerful happened.

Stripped of our usual defenses and coping mechanisms, we become more receptive to forces beyond ourselves. Call it divine intervention, universal energy, or simply the wisdom that comes with stillness, I wasn't relying on my own strength or logic anymore in that vulnerable state: surrendering with nothing left to give and thus tapping into something greater. Receiving *The Game of Life and How to Play It* during such a fragile time was like being handed a key to a locked door I didn't even know existed, the words resonating with me in a way they might not have if I'd read the book during a happier or more stable time. I was open, raw, and ready to receive its message.

Change came next, subtle at first and then undeniable. Circumstances shifted in ways I couldn't explain. Opportunities appeared out of nowhere. Problems that once felt insurmountable began resolving themselves. It felt as if the universe was conspiring in my favor, and while I was in awe, I also hesitated to share these "miracles" openly. Why? Because even the people closest to me, the ones who loved me, didn't get it.

When I tried to explain the shifts I was experiencing, I could feel their skepticism. Some brushed me off, probably thinking I was imagining things or reading too much into coincidences. It hurt, but I understood. It's sometimes difficult for others to see or understand such profound internal changes—especially if they haven't experienced something similar—which is just how it is, so I took none of it personally.

Despite that, I felt compelled to share the book with others and so gifted it to friends, family, anyone I thought might benefit really, and realized something important soon thereafter. If someone isn't mentally or emotionally in the right place to receive that type of message, it won't land. It simply wouldn't stick. Such a person might skim through the pages and make a polite acknowledgement before putting the book aside, missing its depth entirely.

In relating this to you now, I can tell you that if you're reading these words and they're resonating, it's because you're *ready*: to shift, to heal, to grow. If you're not quite there yet, that's okay too! The right message reaches us when we need it most, not a moment sooner nor later. It all happens at the right time.

Looking back, I'm grateful for that painful period. My personal life was an absolute mess at the time, when a relationship I was sure would flourish into a lifelong commitment suddenly ended and I realized it'd been primarily built on deceit. Underscoring that emptiness was anxiety surrounding how I'd navigate the immigration process necessary to remain in the United States, as I knew returning to Grenada was no longer a viable option. I had seven years of college education—a bachelor's and master's—with nothing to show for it. I felt like I was failing at life. That period cracked me open in ways I never expected and gave me the wherewithal to see the power I had within me all along. It wasn't the book alone that changed my life but instead the combination of timing, surrender, and a willingness to shift my mindset. That's when the magic happened. So, if you're standing at a crossroads and feeling lost or broken, know you're not alone. Even if it doesn't feel like it right now, you have the power to change your story. It starts with your thoughts, words, and intentions and begins the moment you decide you're ready.

Two other books profoundly shifted my energy and understanding as well: *The Alchemist* by Paulo Coelho and *The Seven Spiritual Laws of Success* by Deepak Chopra, both guiding me to a deeper awareness of the universal laws and unseen forces that shape our lives. The former showed me the power of pursuing one's "personal legend," that unique purpose we each hold and the importance of trusting the journey even when it seems uncertain: Coelho's storytelling sharing how the universe conspires in our favor when we truly commit to our dreams. It's actually a book I often reach for if I'm feeling a bit disconnected and relying too much on my own power as it makes me feel grounded quickly. *The Seven Spiritual Laws of Success*, meanwhile, offers practical wisdom rooted in spiritual principles. Deepak Chopra eloquently outlines how success isn't purely about hard work but also aligning with universal laws such as intention, detachment, and the law of giving.

Beyond just an intellectual experience, reading these books spoke to my soul. Absorbing their messages transformed how I thought, felt, and acted, and they became foundational texts that reshaped my understanding of how energy flows through life—my own thoughts, words, and actions feeding into the reality I experience.

Another pivotal book that stuck with me is Tony Robbins' *Awaken the Giant Within*. I first picked it up around 2008, and a few specific pages left an indelible mark on me. I vividly recall how on page 175, for example, I was tasked with creating a list—LIST OF WAYS TO CHANGE HOW I FEEL, TO GO FROM PAIN TO PLEASURE, AND TO FEEL GOOD IMMEDIATELY— mentioning 25 things that brought me pleasure. My top five? 1. Exercising. 2. Dancing. 3. Going to the park. 4. Going to a good restaurant. 5. Going to the beach. I remember listing them out one by one, committed to finding activities that worked for me as my first real attempt to consciously manage my emotional state. Skimming through the book now, I'm taken on a parallel emotional journey as it's filled with hand-written notes and dates: a time capsule in its own right.

Page 293, all about PERSONAL DEVELOPMENT GOALS, also stood out. My first goal was to become fluent in French, Spanish, and Italian, something I've yet to achieve. The second? Learn how to salsa and tango by the end of July 2008, my desire to achieve this goal quite literally changing my life. I'd jotted down these goals while on the redeye from Las Vegas in New York on May 22, 2008. Waking up later that morning back home in Medford, NY, I searched for salsa classes in NYC and found one that same evening at 5 pm. Though my exhausted body was screaming at me to go back to bed, the voice in my head said, *Heather, you're single, and salsa is a goal. Mr. Right isn't going to come knocking on your door in Medford. You need to get yourself to the city because you literally just committed to this goal. GO.* I obeyed.

After class, I walked across town and found myself in Murray Hill while looking for a place to eat dinner. Though I couldn't locate the restaurant I was initially searching for, I wound up at another one where a person sitting outside struck up a conversation and raved about the food. One glass of wine and 17 years later, Murray Hill is my home and the man I spoke to is my husband. You can see why *Awaken the Giant Within* would always hold a special place in my heart, my life in that moment underscoring the value of the recommended exercises. Taking the time to chart out where you've been, where you are now, and where you want to go isn't just about goal-setting but also acknowledging that you're seeking meaningful change and are willing to do the work to achieve your goals by taking action.

When I was working as an environmental consultant back in the early 2000s but unsure of where I was headed or what I truly wanted to do, I filled this void of uncertainty with learning. More specifically, I'd frequent the library to borrow audiobooks on CD. Jim Rohn and Earl Nightingale both had programs that made a huge impact on me, each set about 24 CDs—a true commitment—I absorbed voraciously. As my job required driving all over New York and New Jersey, upstate and then back down to Staten Island and Brooklyn and everywhere in between, I used this time to immerse myself in their teachings. Listening to Jim Rohn's timeless philosophies on personal development and Earl Nightingale's *The Strangest Secret* planted the seeds for necessary mindset shifts: Rohn emphasizing the power of discipline and consistency and Nightingale's message ("We become what we think about") resonating deeply.

Looking back now, I realize what a journey it's been: 22 years of evolving, growing, falling, and rising again. I say this not to discourage you but for the sake of transparency. Just because it took me over two decades to land where I am, though, that doesn't necessarily mean it will take *you* that long. Personal growth and transformation are unique to each of us and not a straight line from A to B; it's a winding road but one filled with lessons.

One thing I know for sure is that *thoughts* become *things*, an idea reinforced over and over again through the years as part of an evolution that's by no means abrupt. I didn't go from where I was in 2003 to where I am now overnight, no magic switch to get me there. It was a legitimate, sometimes messy, journey. One key advantage you likely have now that I lacked back then is life experience, something you can use to reflect on past mistakes, learn from them, and move forward with wisdom. Remember: you're not starting from where I was then but instead from where we both are now.

I often say it's not about *whether* we fall but rather *how* we do so. Like I mentioned earlier, if you fall forward, and can see where you're going you can adjust course. Fall backward, and you can get up so long as you can look up. Falling, therefore isn't the enemy; staying down is. Your past doesn't define your future just as your mistakes don't determine your worth. Failure, likewise, isn't an identity but instead a moment in time—every misstep a lesson, every stumble an opportunity to grow.

Another life-changing book I simply must mention is *The Power of Intention* by Dr. Wayne Dyer. I've always been drawn to his work, especially his PBS programs where he speaks about the transformative power of intention. Dr. Dyer taught me that intention isn't just about setting goals but also aligning your energy with your purpose and trusting the universe to meet you halfway. His philosophy of co-creating one's life with a higher power has stayed with me ever since.

I've also found profound inspiration more recently in Gabrielle Bernstein's *The Universe Has Your Back*, a book that arrived in my life at a critical moment—right before my 40th birthday, right smack in the middle of one of the lowest points I'd ever experienced. Not only was my business failing miserably despite my best efforts, but I was unhappy. What was supposed to be a milestone birthday and a joyous occasion instead felt like one of the worst days of my life. I remember thinking, *How did I get here?*

With only about four or five days left in my 30s, I started listening to *The Universe Has Your Back* on Audible and took inspiration from one of the most impactful lessons Bernstein shares therein: the practice of asking the universe for a sign when faced with a big decision. Dragonflies were such a sign for Bernstein, and I decided to try it out for myself.

Before heading out to take my dog for a walk in the park, I was browsing my laptop when I came across a Facebook ad for a coach offering the exact type of guidance I myself had been seeking. I mentioned this earlier, when I shared the importance of creating content that connects. Beyond a coincidence, it felt *intentional*. So there I was, walking through Central Park, listening to Bernstein's book, and reflecting on its message about asking for signs. These tranquil Manhattan grounds have always been a sanctuary for me, a place where I can think clearly and connect with nature. On that particular day, I felt a sense of clarity and peace I hadn't felt in months and decided to hire the aforementioned coach thanks to Bernstein's example—trusting the universe to guide me toward the next step.

A couple of days later, I spoke to her (on my birthday, in fact) over the phone. When she told me her price, I gasped and then immediately started to laugh. "Should I be worried?" she asked with a chuckle herself, hearing what must've sounded like the laughter of an unhinged person on the other end of the line. I uttered the most honest statement ever in response: "I don't know how I'm going to pay you, but I do know my business will absolutely fail if I don't do this." There was no middle ground, and I realized I could decide to walk away (and if it failed, it failed); but if I signed on and it failed anyway, at least I'd know in my soul I did everything I could. I was flying to Los Angeles the following day and told her I'd call back with my decision the day after that.

Back to the book and looking for signs, some type of wink from the universe to avoid being miserable and broke too. I needed to do something. I needed a miracle. Steering clear of anything ambiguous— especially in New York, the capital of the world with no room for doubt—I chose London as my sign. Don't ask me why! I just figured, *Okay, I'm in the United States. What's the likelihood anything about London will just randomly pop up? If it does, that's surely a sign, right?*

Out in LA (Beverly Hills, to be exact) and walking my dog, I found myself desperately searching for grass so she could relieve herself in what was apparently a concrete jungle. We walked for what felt like forever before finally finding a patch. Glancing up, she gave me

213

a look as if to say, "Could you please give me some privacy and turn around?"

Doing just that and looking down Hollywood Boulevard for as far as the eye could see, I suddenly spotted signs on flag poles advertising an exhibition at the Getty Museum; and just what was the name of said exhibition? *London's Calling*. Talk about a sign! It was a miracle. Had we remained in New York, I have no idea how the message would've been delivered; I just know I had asked, and the universe answered with a sign inviting me to make what would ultimately become one of the absolute best decisions I've ever made professionally.

This all simply speaks to a mindset and perspective shift. Take the time to cultivate your mind, putting in everything you'd like to receive and reserving some for the universe too—and if you're a walker like me (or even if you're not!), listen to podcasts that are inspirational and offer value. Consider it a period of fertility, nourishing and enriching your mind knowing nothing can grow on barren land. Let's make the soil therefore as fertile as possible.

CONCLUSION

THE FOUR PILLARS

In our final chapter together, I want to offer you something lasting you can return to time and time again especially on days when doubt creeps in or the road ahead feels unclear.

Let's take a moment to return your awareness to the foundation, the four pillars upon which my own table is built. These pillars are my steady anchors, my personal truths, and my guiding compass as I navigate both life and business. While your journey may look different from mine—as it should—I share these with you not as rules but as reference points. You may find you need more than four pillars to hold your table steady, or perhaps fewer! The beauty of this work is that it's entirely your own. Your table is yours to design, and it should reflect your values, your vision, and the kind of life you're creating.

As I've continued to evolve—personally, professionally, and spiritually—I've realized these four principles show up in my life time and again. Whether I'm making a tough decision, pivoting in business, or simply trying to ground myself during chaotic seasons, I find myself coming back to them almost daily. They are the root of my resilience and the blueprint for building a purpose-driven life and a purpose-driven business.

This final chapter is both a reflection and a resource, a place you can revisit when you need a reset, a reminder, or a little reassurance. Consider it your personal checkpoint, a space to realign with your why, refocus your energy, and reignite your confidence. Because even after the most transformative journey, moments of uncertainty and tests will persist—and that's okay! Not a one-time discovery, purpose is a lifelong commitment. When life tries to pull you away from your vision, these pillars can help bring you back home.

Let's explore them together, one final time.

Pillar One: Trust your intuition.

It's there for a reason. Think of those times when that little voice inside your head speaks up amidst a gut feeling, discomfort, and dis-ease hinting that something's not right—but you don't listen. Why?

Because you decide to rely on logic instead, deeming this a more reasonable path yet regretting it every single time. Work on trusting your intuition. As with any other muscle, not giving it the exercise it needs means it won't sustain you in the way you want it to.

Now, I understand this may be a bit uncomfortable if you're not a person who relies on or believes in intuition. Maybe going down this road feels irrational and like it doesn't make sense even though everything in your being is sending you signals, yet you'd rather ignore them. Here's my advice. Why don't you work on making an intellectual decision but follow it up with your gut? Perhaps that feels a tad better? If you're not comfortable, make whatever decision feels right at that moment. I hope it does indeed work out, but in the event it does not, I'd suggest building that muscle by trusting your intuition when it comes to smaller things moving forward.

I always say that in life, the little things are the big things and how you do one thing is how you do everything. Those are very much my own personal mantras. If you're just starting out and want to do more, really believing you can trust your intuition, how about starting with smaller decisions? Something like, *Okay, if I completely intuit this and it's wrong for any reason, I won't feel as if anything has been lost I can't sort out on my own.* After you do this and flex that muscle a few times, I'd then encourage you to work on trusting your intuition with

217

respect to bigger things—because that's where it matters most, with lessons that are often the most painful should we not learn them.

Pillar Two: What is your why?

Your *why* is your motivator. It's the heartbeat of everything you create and the force that drives you forward when excitement fades and challenges arise. It's also what draws people to your message—not just about what you do but *why* you do it. In a world overflowing with options, people connect with purpose more than products. Your why is what makes your work meaningful, not just for you but for others who see themselves in your journey.

Your why is what gets you out of bed in the morning, especially on the days when things feel heavy, overwhelming, or uncertain. It's the fuel that keeps your fire burning when the grind is *real* or you're tempted to walk away.

Now, let's be honest: it's easy to get swept up in the desire to build a business solely for financial gain, and yes, making money matters. Profit allows you to reinvest, expand your impact, and create freedom. If *money* is your only reason for building, however, I can assure you burnout is just around the corner. Because what happens once you hit that financial goal and finally "make it"? With no deeper mission beneath the surface, you'll quickly find yourself stuck, disillusioned, and disconnected. You'll feel it, and so will the people around you. Without a strong why, there's no anchor to keep it all from drifting away.

On the other hand, when your why is rooted in solving real problems, meeting real needs, and doing work that reflects your values and purpose, it becomes a *sustainable source of energy* as something bigger than you—something people want to support, be part of, and help carry forward. That kind of mission not only fuels you, but it attracts aligned customers, collaborators, and community members who believe in what you're building.

Your why helps you create more than just a brand. It helps you build a *movement*. When you're fueled by purpose, not just profit, everything becomes more meaningful: your messaging, your products, your decisions, your resilience. You're no longer just selling—you're serving. You're not just launching—you're leading.

So, I invite you to go deeper than surface goals and ask yourself:

- What is the real reason I'm doing this?

- What do I care deeply about changing, healing, creating, or improving in the world?

- What challenge(s) do I feel uniquely called to solve?

219

Your answers to these questions are the foundation of your why. When you lead with it, your business becomes more than a source of income as a vehicle for impact; and that, my friend, is where real fulfillment lives.

Pillar 3: Don't let your destination become your limitation.

This pillar is one I've touched on before and intentionally so—because it's a stumbling block that trips up far too many people on their path to purpose. When we set out on our journeys, we typically have a clear idea of where we want to go. We create a vision, we set goals, we chart a path. While having direction is powerful and necessary, it can become a double-edged sword if we're not careful. Here's what I mean...

In becoming so attached to the destination, we often miss unexpected opportunities that show up along the way: gripping onto our original plan so tightly that we fa l to see the better one trying so hard to reveal itself. Life, in all its unpredictability, rarely follows the script we write in our heads. Pitfalls, pivots, and detours are not exceptions—they're part of the process. When things don't go as planned, we tend to panic and interpret setbacks as signs of failure. We assume we're off track, but the truth is, *every challenge is a classroom*. Every hurdle is an invitation to build resilience, refine our skills, and discover new possibilities we hadn't even considered.

I want to encourage you to look at every obstacle not just as a problem but as a potential seed from which great things grow, knowing there's something powerful in cultivating the mindset that setbacks are simply set*ups* for what's next. Each problem you solve sharpens your critical thinking. Each "failure" reveals a lesson you didn't know you needed. Each closed door teaches you how to unlock and open it—or even build a door of your own!

As you move forward, you're not just heading toward a destination; you're becoming someone brand-new. Stronger. Wiser. More capable. This evolution is just as important as reaching the original goal, if not even more so.

It's so easy to feel discouraged when the journey doesn't play out how you'd originally imagined it, but growth rarely happens in a straight line. Sometimes, the most extraordinary outcomes arise from these apparent "detours." When you stay open—mentally, emotionally, and spiritually—you create space for possibility and begin to align with opportunities matching your deeper purpose, not just your original plan.

So yes, hold your vision close, but hold it *lightly*. Take aligned action. Do the work. Stay committed. Allow space for unfolding, and let life show you what it has in store. More often than not, what's waiting on the other side of flexibility is far greater than what you could have planned alone.

Your destination is, of course, important—but don't let it limit what's possible. Stay open. Stay curious. Above all else, trust that your path is unfolding exactly as it should even if it looks nothing like what you originally expected.

Because sometimes, your greatest expansion lies just outside the boundaries of the original blueprint.

Pillar Four: The questions you ask are the problems you solve.

If your goal is to lead a purpose-driven business and live a purpose-driven life, you'll absolutely flow best while living in service of others. Ask yourself: *What problems am I solving? What challenges are people actually experiencing? How can that gift, that thing aligning me with my assignment, actually help tackle others' challenges?* In doing so, two things happen. You first begin to gain clarity on who your client is—because in life and in business, you can't be everything to everybody. You can then double down on your ideal customer. *What problems do they have, and how can I help solve them?* Asking these questions helps pinpoint the challenges you'll solve to connect and really just go further faster thanks to this clarity—which comes from taking action, not thinking thoughts. Once you understand who that community is and how you can solve the problems they're experiencing, you're absolutely able to serve: the foundation of living a purpose-driven life and owning a purpose-driven business.

For so much of my life, it felt as if I was stuck on the local train—everyone else on the express. Things I wanted seemingly took forever, feelings of doubt and insufficiency often creeping in during this time. As I hustled during those years, the vision I had for my life and knowledge gleaned from literally hundreds of self-help books sustained me. Twenty-one years later, my life now looks a lot like the vision boards I created back then. The most interesting part? I'm still evolving and growing, embracing a new vision and acquiring the skills necessary to achieve my life's evolution.

If you have a vision for your own life, it's never too late—which is precisely why I embarked on my journey to provide women in particular with the guidance, support, and tools necessary to pivot into the lives they envision for themselves. Don't let fear rob you of your best season. There's one thing that I know with absolute certainty: If you don't believe you're worthy of any of this or that your goals and dreams can materialize, in both cases you will be right. It's absolutely critical to prepare your mind.

I also know what it feels like to feel so low you have to reach up to touch bottom, as if everything in life is working against you. You've done everything you were told to do. You've followed the rules, checked all the boxes, and done your part. You've worked hard, displayed kindness, stayed patient, and maybe even sacrificed parts of yourself along the way. You've been the reliable one, the one others can count on. Despite all of this, though, you seem to always end up with the short end of the stick.

I know how it feels, the heaviness that comes with wondering why something isn't working or what exactly you're doing wrong. I know how easy it is for the voice in your head to whisper doubts and tell you you're not good enough, not smart enough, not worthy enough. That negative self-talk is relentless. It sneaks in quietly at first, but before you know it, your head is in your hands trying to silence the noise.

I've been there and experienced moments when I questioned everything: my path, my abilities, my worth. I've fallen prey to that dark space where self-doubt lingers and whispers nothing will ever change and that maybe I was foolish to dream of something more. It's a tough place to be, I can tell you that! It's exhausting, lonely, and as if you're trapped in a cycle you can't break free from. Guess what, though? None of it is true! The voice you consider your protector is actually more of a thief, set to steal everything of value in your soul while you're not paying attention.

It took me a long time to understand this, but the truth is, nothing in your life will change until you change the story you're telling yourself. The narrative playing on a loop in your mind is powerful, shaping your choices, your confidence, and your resilience. If you keep telling yourself that you're stuck, that you're not worthy, or that success is something reserved for "other people," it will inevitably become your reality.

The opposite is also true, however.

When you begin to rewrite that narrative and *believe* you're worthy, capable, and deserve a life filled with purpose and joy, things begin to shift. Doors once seemingly closed start to open, and opportunities once seemingly out of reach start to appear. Most importantly, you begin to realize you don't need anyone else's permission to pursue the life you want.

The fact that you're here and reading these words tells me something powerful: that deep down, you already believe there's still a chance for you. A chance to break free from the cycle you've been stuck in, create something that's yours, and finally live the life you've dreamed about for so long.

That spark inside you? The one that inspired you to pick up this book and stick with it to the very end? That spark is *real*. It's your intuition and higher self, reminding you you're meant for more and that it's not too late. It's never too late. Here's the thing about that spark, though; it needs your attention to stay alive. You must believe in it, protect it, and feed it with positive thoughts and bold action. Because if you don't, the noise of the world—all the doubts, fears, and endless list of "shoulds"—will try to snuff it out.

So, let me remind you: You are enough. You are worthy. You are capable.

You don't need someone else to offer you a seat at their table nor to wait for an invitation or the perfect moment to arrive. *You* have the power to create your own table, one built on your dreams, values, and vision for the life you want to live. Most importantly, this table will allow you to serve others; there's no purpose without service, after all.

Building your own table isn't always easy. There will be challenges and days when you question if you're on the right path. There will be moments when fear tries to convince you to go back to what's safe and familiar. I promise you this, though; every step you take toward building something authentically yours is worth it. Every risk, every late night, every moment of uncertainty: all lead you closer to the life you deserve. And the best part? You don't have to go it alone.

I'm here with you, cheering you on, supporting you, and reminding you of your strength every step of the way. I know what it's like to feel stuck, to feel small, to feel like your dreams are just out of reach; but I also know what it feels like to break free from those thoughts and reclaim your power as you build something beautiful from the ground up.

I want that for *you*.

I didn't write this book to provide tools and strategies— though I hope you found plenty of those along the way— but instead to remind you that you already have what it takes. You always have. Sometimes, all it takes is a little nudge and reminder that we're more powerful than we realize.

As you step forward into the next chapter of your life, carry this truth with you. You are the author of your story and have the power to decide what comes next, with the strength to rewrite the parts that no longer serve you and create an exciting future. Moreover, you have the courage to take the first step, however small, toward building the life you truly want.

No more waiting. No more shrinking yourself to fit into spaces not built for you. It's time to dream bigger, step into your power, and create your own table reflecting your worth, your vision, and your limitless potential.

Remember: I'm here with you, every step of the way.

Let's build something incredible together.

ACKNOWLEDGEMENTS

This book came to life under an intense and ambitious timeline, demanding long days, late nights, and unwavering focus. I am incredibly grateful to those who stood beside me throughout this journey.

To my husband, Amos—thank you for your constant support and belief in me. Your unwavering love, patience, and encouragement continue to be the foundation that allows me to pursue my passions fully. None of this would be possible without you.

To Sharon Dariels, my gifted photographer—thank you for capturing such a stunning cover image and for walking alongside me on this journey of authorship. Your creativity and your introduction to the world of lifestyle modeling have been unexpected gifts that I deeply cherish.

To my editor, Kerri—your ability to meet my fast-paced deadlines without compromising quality was nothing short of extraordinary. Your flexibility and dedication gave me the confidence that this book would make it to the finish line on time.

To the incredible team at Edge Voice Over Studio—thank you for coming together so quickly and professionally to help bring this project across the finish line. Your commitment made a meaningful impact in helping me meet my release date.

To my coaches, teachers, family, and friends—none of this would be possible without you. Each of you, in your own way, has poured into me. You've provided the foundation upon which I've been able to build an extraordinary life, and I do not take that for granted.

And finally, to my readers—this book was written for you. When the stirring began within me, urging me to write these words, it came with a sense of urgency I couldn't ignore. I don't do things just to check a box. I do them because I believe in them, and because I want to make a genuine difference.

I didn't waste a moment—because I know how suffocating it can feel when even one more minute feels like a minute too long. This is for you. I hope something in these pages stirred your spirit, sparked your courage, and inspired you to take the first step in creating your own table.

Everything you need is already within you.

CREATE YOUR OWN TABLE WORKBOOK

A Companion to Help You Discover, Clarify, and Act on Your Purpose

Welcome Message from the Author

Congratulations on reaching this point in your journey. You didn't just read this book—you experienced it. You've explored ideas that challenge the status quo, invited your intuition to speak up, and dared to believe there's more for you. This workbook is your invitation to take action and put what you've read into practice. Your purpose isn't something to find—it's something to *live*. Let's build your table, one meaningful pillar at a time.

How to Use This Workbook

- Be honest. There are no wrong answers.
- Come back to these pages often. Growth isn't linear.
- Use additional paper or a journal as needed.
- Give yourself permission to dream *and* do.
- This is sacred space. Treat it with care.

✦ Section 1: Looking Back to Move Forward

Prompt 1:

What moments in your life stand out as defining? These could be times of triumph or challenge.

→ *Write down three and note what each taught you about yourself.*

1. _____

2. _____

3. _____

Prompt 2:

What patterns or themes do you notice in the roles you've played (personally or professionally) over the years?

→ *What do these patterns tell you about your natural gifts or unmet needs?*

1. _____

2. _____

3. _____

4. _____

5. _____

✦ Section 2: Redefining Your Truth

Prompt 3:

What beliefs have you inherited that you're now beginning to question?
→ *List at least three. Then next to each, write: "Is this true for me?"*

1._____

2._____

3. _____

Prompt 4:

Who were you before the world told you who to be?
→ *Reflect on your childhood interests, dreams, and instincts.*

1. _____

2. _____

3. _____

✦ Section 3: Asking Better Questions

The questions you ask determine the direction of your clarity.

Prompt 5:
Instead of asking, "Why me?" try asking:
→ *"What is this moment trying to teach me?"*
Write about a recent experience that left you feeling stuck or uncertain. Now reframe it by asking a better question.

1. _____

2. _____

3. _____

4. _____

5. _____

Prompt 6:
List 3 questions you need to start asking yourself more often to move forward.

1. _____

2. _____

3. _____

✦ Section 4: Intuition and Alignment

Prompt 7:

When have you ignored your intuition—and what was the outcome?

1. _____

2. _____

3. _____

Now, when have you *followed* it? What happened?

1. _____

2. _____

3. _____

Prompt 8:

What would it look like to live in alignment with what feels right for you—not just what looks right to others?

1. _____

2. _____

3. _____

✦ Section 5: Your Purpose & Personal Brand

Prompt 9:
How do you define "purpose" in this season of your life?

1. _____

2. _____

3. _____

4. _____

Prompt 10:
If someone asked, "What do you stand for?"—what would you say?

1. _____

2. _____

3. _____

4. _____

Prompt 11:
What impact do you want to leave behind?

1. _____

2. _____

3. _____

4. _____

5. _____

How can your story become someone else's permission slip?

1. _____

2. _____

3. _____

4. _____

5. _____

✦ Section 6: Action Begins With Clarity

You don't need to have it all figured out—just take the next right step.

Prompt 12:
What's one thing you can do this week that aligns with the person you are becoming?

1. _____

Prompt 13:
What support do you need (community, coaching, time, tools) to take action?

1. _____

2. _____

3. _____

4. _____

Prompt 14:
What will you no longer tolerate as you move forward?

1. _____

2. _____

3. _____

4. _____

✦ Section 7: Your Table, Your Terms

Prompt 15:
What kind of table are you building?
→ *Describe what it looks like, who you want at it, and what values it's grounded in.*

Response:

Prompt 16:
If this table is a reflection of who you truly are, what parts of you still need permission to show up?

1. _____

2. _____

3. _____

4. _____

5. _____

"This section is grounded in the Four Pillars. Since the questions are designed to spark deeper reflection, a journal is the ideal place to capture your thoughts and discoveries."

Pillar 1: INTUITION

"Your inner voice is the first architect of your purpose."

Self-Reflection Prompts

- What messages or nudges have you been ignoring lately?

- What would trusting yourself more look like in your everyday life?

- What are three decisions you've been postponing that intuition could guide?

Deep Dive Exercise: Body Compass

Think back to a moment when your body told you something was off.

- What were the signals? (e.g., tight chest, stomach drop)
  Now think of a time you felt fully aligned.

- What did that feel like? (e.g., calm, excited, energized)

My body says "yes" when…
My body says "no" when…

Intuitive Action Plan

Choose one decision area (career, relationship, health, etc.).
Write a pros and cons list based only on your *intuition*, not logic.
What is your gut leading you to do?

Affirmation

I trust the wisdom within me. My intuition leads me to truth, alignment, and purpose.

Pillar 2: WHAT IS YOUR WHY?

"When you know your why, your how shows up."

Clarity Journal Prompts

- What do I love doing—even when I'm not getting paid?

- When do I feel most alive, most myself, most fulfilled?

- What legacy do I want to leave behind?

Impact Mapping Exercise

Use the circles below to map your impact:

What I love → What I'm good at → What people need → What I can be paid for
(Use this to help define your *zone of purpose*.)

Guided Visualization: Meet Your Future Self

Close your eyes and imagine yourself five years from now, fully living in your purpose.

- What are you doing?

- Who are you helping?

- How do you feel at the end of each day?
  Write down what you saw and felt.

Affirmation

My purpose is the fire that lights my path. I am here for a reason, and I honor it with every step I take.

Pillar 3: THE QUESTIONS YOU ASK ARE THE PROBLEMS YOU SOLVE

"Your questions reveal your purpose. Your answers reveal your power."

Problem-Solving Prompts

- What challenges have I overcome that others still face?
- What topic could I speak about for 30 minutes with no prep?
- What problem would I gladly wake up early or stay up late to solve?

The Purpose Triangle

Label each point:

- What people come to me for
- What I've lived through and learned
- What I care deeply about

Where they intersect is the question you were born to answer.

Case Study Exercise: Your Journey as the Blueprint

Think of a turning point in your life.

- What problem did you face?
- What question did you have?
- How did you solve it?
  Now imagine turning that journey into a service, talk, or offer.

Affirmation

I carry answers forged by experience and compassion. I solve problems that matter because I've lived them.

Pillar 4: DON'T LET YOUR DESTINATION BECOME YOUR LIMITATION

"Every end is a beginning in disguise."

Release & Redefine Journaling

- What goals have you outgrown?

- What titles or identities are you afraid to let go of?

- Who might you become if you weren't afraid to start over?

The Roadmap Remix Exercise

Draw a timeline of your life. Mark every "detour" moment.

- What did you learn?

- What unexpected doors opened?

- How did your direction shift for the better?

Now rewrite your future from the perspective of *possibility*, not *predictability*.

New Destination Declaration

I give myself permission to pivot. The path is mine to create. I am not defined by one outcome—I am empowered by every next step.

Build Your Table: Integration & Action

Your Four Pillars, Personalized

PILLAR	What This Means to Me	How I Will Practice This
Intuition		
My Why		
Questions I Solve		
No Limit Destination		

Design Your Table (Visual or Written)

Draw, sketch, or write a metaphorical description of your custom table—your purpose platform. Include what each leg stands for and what you'll place on top (your mission, brand, career, life, etc.).

Final Activation: Purpose in Motion

Write Your Purpose Declaration

I am here to

_____

by _____

for those who

_____

30-Day Purpose Plan

Set one goal in each category below:

- **Mindset Shift:**

- **Daily Habit:**

- **Connection/Outreach:**

- **Creative/Business Action:**

- **Self-Care Practice:**

Closing Encouragement

This is your table. Your space. Your seat.
You no longer need permission. You've already started.
The world is waiting for what only you can bring. Show
up fully—and own it.

ABOUT THE AUTHOR

Heather Dolland Tamam is a serial entrepreneur, author, speaker, transition coach, and business strategist dedicated to empowering individuals, especially professionals seeking career transitions and aspiring entrepreneurs. She is the founder of Doltam Creative Solutions (MWBE), a company that helps women who feel undervalued in unfulfilling careers take control of their futures by building businesses and personal brands that reflect their true passions.

As an author, Heather has written multiple books, including:

- *Create Your Own Table – A guide for professionals transitioning from corporate careers to entrepreneurship (May 2025 Release)*

- *Pivot Because Life Doesn't Always Go As Planned - A practical guide for navigating unexpected changes in career, business, and life.*

- *Discovering the New York Craft Spirits Boom – An exploration of the rise of the craft spirits industry.*

- *Before The Glass Things to Consider When Entering the Booze Business - A blueprint for*

> *anyone interested in entering the alcohol business*

- *The Quick Author Formula – A step-by-step system for writing and publishing a book in weeks, not years. (e-book)*

You can contact Heather by visiting www.doltam.com or the following social media platforms:

Youtube

www.youtube.com/@heatherdollandtamam

Instagram

instagram.com/doltamsolutions

LinkedIn

linkedin.com/in/heatherdollandtamam

www.ingramcontent.com/pod-product-compliance
Lightning Source LLC
Chambersburg PA
CBHW051510120626
46551CB00012B/863